THE ULTIMATE GUIDE TO THE
JUSTICE LEAGUE OF AMERICA

LONDON, NEW YORK, MUNICH,
MELBOURNE, and DELHI

Senior Editor Alastair Dougall
Senior Designer Robert Perry
Designers Guy Harvey, Dan Bunyan,
Nick Avery
Publishing Manager Mary Atkinson
Art Director Cathy Tincknell
Production Nicola Torode
DTP Designer Jill Bunyan

03 04 05 06 10 9 8 7 6 5 4 3

Published in the United States by
DK Publishing, Inc., 375 Hudson Street, New York, NY 10014

DK Publishing, Inc. offers special discounts for bulk purchases for sales promotions or premiums.
Specific, large-quantity needs can be met with special editions, including personalized covers, excerpts
of existing guides, and corporate imprints. For more information, contact Special Markets Department,
DK Publishing, Inc., 375 Hudson Street, New York, NY 10014 Fax: 800-600-9098.

Library of Congress Cataloging-in-Publication Data
The ultimate guide to the Justice League of America / [author, Scott
Beatty ; illustrator, Roger Stewart].-- 1st American ed.
p. cm.
Summary: Introduces the characters--heroes and villains--and major story
lines of DC Comics' comic books about the interplanetary club of
superheroes who work together to safeguard the universe.
ISBN 0-7894-8893-0
1. Justice League of America (Comic strip) 2. Justice League of
America (Fictitious characters) [1. Justice League of America (Comic
strip) 2. Cartoons and comics.] I. Beatty, Scott, 1969- II. Stewart,
Roger, ill.
PN6728.J87 U45 2002
741.5'973--dc21
2002073387

Color reproduction by Media Development and Printing Ltd., UK
Printed and bound in Spain by Artes Graficas, Toledo

Visit DC Comics online at www.dccomics.com or at keyword DC Comics on America Online.

see our complete product line at
www.dk.com

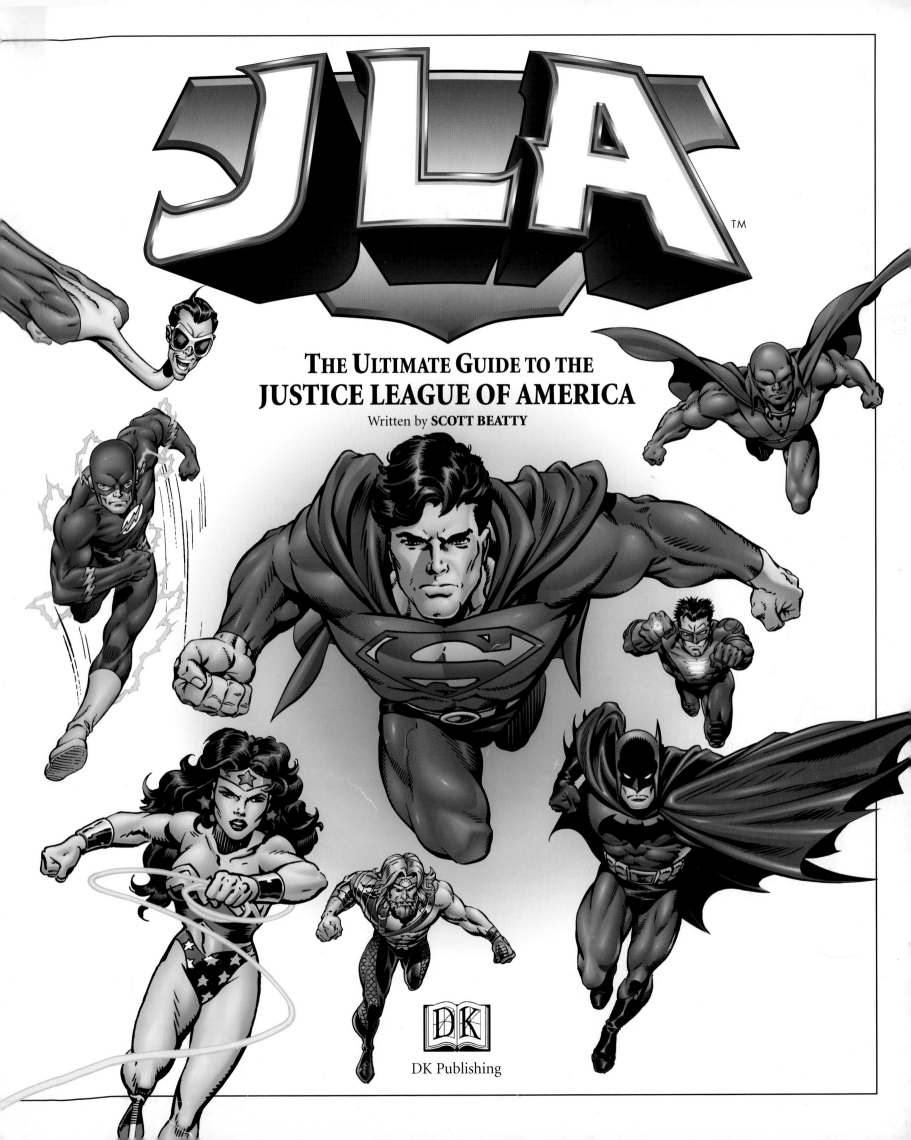

JLA™

THE ULTIMATE GUIDE TO THE
JUSTICE LEAGUE OF AMERICA

Written by SCOTT BEATTY

DK Publishing

CONTENTS

MEMBERS OF THE LEAGUE

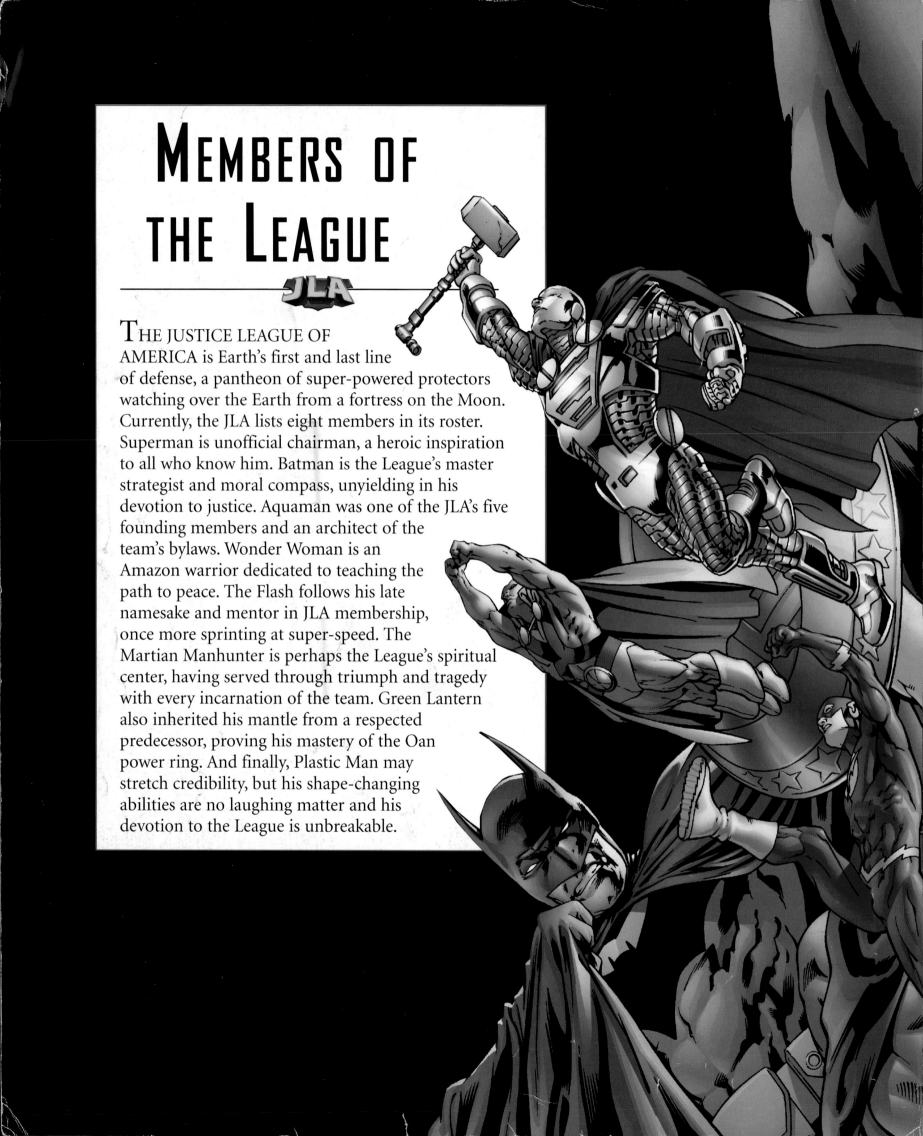

THE JUSTICE LEAGUE OF AMERICA is Earth's first and last line of defense, a pantheon of super-powered protectors watching over the Earth from a fortress on the Moon. Currently, the JLA lists eight members in its roster. Superman is unofficial chairman, a heroic inspiration to all who know him. Batman is the League's master strategist and moral compass, unyielding in his devotion to justice. Aquaman was one of the JLA's five founding members and an architect of the team's bylaws. Wonder Woman is an Amazon warrior dedicated to teaching the path to peace. The Flash follows his late namesake and mentor in JLA membership, once more sprinting at super-speed. The Martian Manhunter is perhaps the League's spiritual center, having served through triumph and tragedy with every incarnation of the team. Green Lantern also inherited his mantle from a respected predecessor, proving his mastery of the Oan power ring. And finally, Plastic Man may stretch credibility, but his shape-changing abilities are no laughing matter and his devotion to the League is unbreakable.

SUPERMAN
JLA

ROCKETED TO EARTH from the doomed planet Krypton, the infant Kal-El grew tall and strong under the rays of Earth's yellow sun. The Kents, kindly Kansas farmers, adopted Kal-El, christened him Clark, and raised him to believe in truth, justice, and the American way. By his teens, Clark had developed miraculous superpowers. As a young adult, Clark left Smallville High for the excitement of big-city Metropolis, where the press dubbed him "Superman" when he single-handedly saved a crashing space-plane. Ever since, this Man of Steel has become Earth's most beloved and trusted hero!

REAL NAME Clark Kent

OCCUPATION
Super Hero/Journalist

BASE Metropolis

HEIGHT 6 ft 3 in

WEIGHT 225 lb

EYES Blue HAIR Black

FIRST APPEARANCE
ACTION COMICS #1
(June 1938)

CHAIRMAN OF THE BOARD
Superman first declined JLA membership because of his many responsibilities elsewhere. With the JLA's recent restructuring, however, he has virtually led the team, thanks to his revered status within Earth's superhuman community.

SUPERPOWERS
In addition to super-strength sufficient to move mountains, the Man of Steel can fly at tremendous speeds and is virtually invulnerable to injury. His super-senses include X-ray and heat vision, flash-freezing super-breath, and super-hearing.

CLARK KENT
Clark is a foreign correspondent for the Metropolis-based *Daily Planet*, where his wife – Pulitzer Prize-winning journalist Lois Lane Kent – is also employed. Lois knows all about her husband's super alter ego. She often helps to cover for his sudden absences from work when an emergency hits and he takes to the air with the words: "This is a job for Superman!"

LOIS, I WAS ABOUT TO RESPOND TO A JLA EMERGENCY...

HIS WORLD AT WAR

On his own, Superman has saved the planet countless times. Once, however, the Man of Steel faced an enemy so immense that all Earth's heroes were called into action, joining together to fend off the world-shattering Imperiex. Despite his own herculean efforts, Superman could not spare everyone from pitiless Imperiex-Probes. Wonder Woman's mother, Hippolyta, fell in battle, as did many other heroic souls. Even Aquaman was believed missing in action for a time. But in the end, the Man of Steel marshaled all of his strength and resolve to save his adopted world once more during its darkest hour.

ULTRA-VIOLENT LIGHT

When Batman studied his JLA teammates to determine their weaknesses, he knew that defeating Superman – short of killing him with green kryptonite – would involve totally incapacitating the Man of Steel. Eco-terrorist Rā's al Ghūl put the Dark Knight's theories to use by exposing Superman to artificial red kryptonite and rendering his skin transparent. Empowering sunlight thus became instantly agonizing to him.

A HERO FALLS

The burden of leadership can be heavy – even for the Man of Steel. Inspired by Superman, the super-powered Mark Antaeus joined the JLA as a reserve member. Antaeus resigned when League policy prohibited him from intervening in a Middle Eastern political crisis. Antaeus's actions led to greater bloodshed and he killed himself from shame.

GREEN DEATH

Superman's solar-charged cells make him nigh-invulnerable, yet one substance is his Achilles' heel. Radioactive fragments of the planet Krypton – kryptonite – can sap Superman's powers and kill him. Realizing this, the White Martians once used their telepathic powers to convince the Man of Steel that he was being tortured by the green-glowing element!

BATMAN

JLA

THE DARK NIGHT DETECTIVE wages a ceaseless crusade to end crime in Gotham City. As a child, Bruce Wayne witnessed the brutal murders of his parents, gunned down by a remorseless robber. Young Bruce swore an oath to avenge their deaths, traveling the world in a decade-long sojourn to hone both his body and mind to the pinnacles of human perfection. Inspired by a bat crashing through his study window, the adult Bruce conceived a mask and mantle sure to strike terror into the hearts of cowardly and superstitious criminals: the fearsome visage of Batman!

MASTER PLANNER

Since he prefers to operate alone or only with his personally trained partners, the Dark Knight seems an unlikely team player. But Batman's keen analytical mind makes him an integral part of the Justice League as its resident strategist, often coordinating the team's counterattacks.

Batman on watch in the JLA Monitor Womb.

Nomex fire-resistant material.

Batman swings through the skyscraper canyons of Gotham on de-cel jumplines.

SECRET SUSPICIONS

In the unlikely event that the Justice League should ever turn against mankind, Batman determined his super-powered teammates' respective weaknesses, secretly formulating fail-safe countermeasures to defeat each one of them.

BRUCE WAYNE

Few Justice Leaguers beyond the eight permanent members know that Bruce Wayne is Batman. Coached by valet Alfred Pennyworth – a former actor on the London stage – Bruce poses as a shallow playboy. Alfred, meanwhile, knows all Bruce's secrets, aiding and abetting the Dark Knight's war on crime while maintaining the illusion of Bruce Wayne, the bored billionaire.

REAL NAME Bru
OCCUPATION Inc
Crime Fig
BASE Gotham
HEIGHT 6 ft
WEIGHT 21
EYES Blue HAI

FIRST APPEARAN
DETECTIVE COMIC
(May 1939)

BATPLANE

To keep pace with League members who can fly unaided, Batman uses a stealthy suborbital jet. Based on various Wayne Aviation prototypes, these single-seater, supersonic Batplanes define the cutting edge of aeronautical development with "smart" missile technology and evasion tactical software.

BAT-WEAPONS

Batman's Utility Belt contains a small arsenal of miniaturized and collapsible non-lethal deterrents, including climbing grapnels, jumplines, gas pellets, electronics gear, aerosol sprays, and his signature Batarangs.

PROMETHEUS DEFEATED!

Batman spent years perfecting every known fighting discipline. But it took Prometheus just seconds to download the Dark Knight's hard-won skills – and those of 29 other martial arts masters – into his cerebral cortex! Prometheus scored first blood, but a humbled Batman later dismantled the villain's computerized helmet and deleted his virtual combat programs. In their second fateful encounter, the Dark Knight soundly defeated his criminal counterpart!

Adding insult to injury, Batman imprinted Prometheus' circuitry with the physical characteristics of motor neuron disease to incapacitate him!

THE WORLD'S FINEST

While they are as different as night is to day, the Caped Crusader and the Last Son of Krypton have built a friendship based on mutual respect for the other despite their philosophical differences. Superman once entrusted Batman alone to safeguard a kryptonite ring deadly to the Man of Steel.

NO MAN'S LAND

They've saved Earth innumerable times, but Gotham City was one problem the JLA couldn't solve. The League was barred by Congressional edict from helping Gotham, victim of a terrible earthquake and abandoned as a federal disaster area. Even Batman agreed that Gotham must rise from its own ruins, putting himself at loggerheads with his frustrated teammates.

Kevlar-lined cape slows impact of bullets.

AQUAMAN

JLA

SOVEREIGN OF THE SEVEN SEAS, Aquaman is ruler of a kingdom covering three-quarters of the Earth's surface. Born to Queen Atlanna of the city Poseidonis, capital of the undersea kingdom of Atlantis, the infant Orin was abandoned by his father, King Trevis, for possessing blond hair, the "Curse of Kordax." In addition to his ancestor's golden locks, Orin possessed Kordax's empathy with sea life, a survival skill that enabled him to be rescued and raised by the dolphin matron Porm!

Lightweight and flexible Atlantean alloy armor.

"Liquid metal" cybernetic hand.

YOUNG ARTHUR
Aged ten, Orin was captured by lighthouse keeper Arthur Curry after the Atlantean youth freed fearful crustaceans from Curry's lobster traps. Slowly, Curry established trust and taught Orin the ways of the surface world as his surrogate father.

APPLE!

KING OF THE SEA

Orin was later abandoned by Curry, who had made the boy his namesake. Arthur Jr. lived among Alaskan Inuit before his heroic exploits earned him the title "Aquaman" from the global media. Although uncomfortable in the surface world, Aquaman helped to form the Justice League. His fellow heroes stood as friends and witnesses at Arthur's marriage to the beautiful red-tressed Mera, aquatic queen from another dimension.

REAL NAME Arthur "Orin" Curry
OCCUPATION King of Atlantis
BASE Poseidonis
HEIGHT 6 ft 1 in
WEIGHT 325 lb
EYES Sea Blue
HAIR Blond
FIRST APPEARANCE
MORE FUN COMICS #73
(November 1941)

CHARYBDIS
The terrorist Charybdis is responsible for the hook that has replaced Aquaman's left hand. After ambushing the Sea King, Charybdis absorbed some of Arthur's aquatic powers, forcing a school of ravenous piranha to devour the limb. Though wracked with agony, Aquaman turned the hungry fish upon their evil master.

PAF

AQUATIC POWERS
Aquaman can survive at great ocean depths. He is able to breathe on land or sea, although he must submerge periodically to replenish his tremendous strength. His greatest power is his ability to telepathically communicate with sea creatures. Aquaman's cybernetic left hand can morph from a metallic prosthetic to a retractable cable-spun harpoon.

CORAL. SUCH A SIMPLE FORM OF LIFE.

BUT IF THE COMMUNITY IS ACTING AS ONE, THEY SHOULD RESPOND TO A TELEPATHIC SIGNAL--

POSEIDONIS

Forty-thousand years ago, the city of Poseidonis – encapsulated by King Orin to shield it from barbarian hordes – sank beneath the waves after the Atlantean continent was struck by a meteor. To survive undersea, the Atlanteans had little recourse but to alter their genetics and become amphibious .

THE PALACE

Erected in the heart of Poseidonis, the palace is home to Aquaman and Queen Mera, as well as the young hero Tempest, his wife, Dolphin, and their infant son, Cerdian. It is also the seat of government for the Atlantean cabinet. The palace and its grounds are well fortified and patrolled by the elite Seahorse Cavalry.

THE RAZING OF ATLANTIS

During the epic Imperiex War, Superman and the JLA battled to prevent Earth's demolition. Tragically, Atlantis was ground zero for the "Hollowing" of the planet to beget a new universe. Aquaman fought valiantly, but – in a battle so furious the ocean itself was parted – the King of the Seas and Atlantis were believed destroyed. In truth, both Aquaman and his beloved city were only lost for a time.

THE AQUACAVE

Aquaman's dry cavern headquarters is located northeast of Poseidonis along the continental shelf. It contains living quarters, a trophy room filled with booty from the sea floor, and a study containing the Atlantis Chronicles, which detail the long and bloody history of the continent and its diverse peoples.

Meditation Gazebo

Atlantean Archives

Royal Palace

Business Quarter

Atlantean dwellings

Council of Worship

Hydros... farms ...w nutrition-rich kelp.

Cabinet Chamber

Royal Reception Hall

Hall of Science

Queen Mera's Hospital

New Town District includes Farmer's Market and Pangaea Institute.

Crystal dome resists tremendous oceanic pressures.

Jeweled, razor-sharp tiara, which once symbolized Diana's royal status, can be hurled like a boomerang.

WONDER WOMAN
JLA

MOLDED FROM CLAY and given life by the goddesses of Greek myth, Diana of Themyscira is a "Wonder Woman" in every way. Made real to thwart the war god Ares, this Amazon princess and warrior was sent beyond her native shores to be an ambassador of peace among humanity. Wonder Woman has lived and died, ascended to *and* forsaken godhood to protect Earth and promote equality among its peoples.

Diana possesses the strength of Gaea the Earth mother.

Gilded battle armor forged by the artisan Pallas.

Hestia's magical, indestructible Lasso of Truth.

REAL NAME Diana
OCCUPATION Ambassador
BASE New York City
HEIGHT 5 ft 11 in
WEIGHT 150 lb
EYES Blue **HAIR** Black
FIRST APPEARANCE
ALL-STAR COMICS #8
(Winter 1941)

HIPPOLYTA'S CHILD
Diana is daughter of the late Queen Hippolyta, who ruled her Amazon sisters wisely for centuries while beseeching her patron goddesses for a child. Hippolyta's prayers were answered when she sculpted a baby from clay and the messenger god Hermes gave the infant life.

THE GODS' GIFTS
Hermes granted Diana speed and the power of flight. The Goddesses of Olympus bestowed their own gifts upon her. From Demeter came the strength of Gaea, Mother Earth. Athena granted wisdom. From Artemis came the eyes of a hunter and oneness with the animal kingdom, while Hestia granted Diana the power to open men's hearts so she might teach them the path to peace.

WONDER WEAPONS
Although matchless with a sword or spear, Diana's most prized weapons are her silver bracelets and Golden Lasso. Able to deflect bullets and generate a small energy shield, Diana's unbreakable Bracelets of Victory were forged from the Aegis of Zeus. Diana's Lasso of Truth, was wrought from the Golden Girdle of Gaea and compels anyone bound by it to speak only the truth.

THEMYSCIRA

Island of Healing

Temple of the Oracle

Coliseum

The Amazons' island paradise is secreted in the Bermuda Triangle. This gravity-defying dimensional gateway has been reconstructed to new heights of glory following the depredations of Darkseid, a civil conflict, and the Imperiex War.

SEE-THROUGH VEHICLES

Diana's amazing translucent transport is the product of a consciousness known as The Ring that once belonged to the sightless alien Lansanarians. Telepathically linked to Diana, this entity can morph into any number of vehicles – including a chariot or Invisible Jet – and even erect an entire fortress, the Wonderdome.

To restore the lasso, Diana embarked on a spirit quest to the Land of Shade, battling many mythical beasts.

GOLDEN PERFECT

When a young boy – next in line to become the country of Jarhanpur's guardian "Rama Khan" – was held against his mother's will, Wonder Woman intervened. But by allowing the boy to remain a virtual slave to Jarhanpur, Wonder Woman compromised her moral code and unraveled her own arbiter of truth, Hestia's Golden Lasso!

SLEEPING BEAUTY

The Queen of Fables may have believed Diana to be Snow White, but she struck her down like Sleeping Beauty, who could not be roused from her deep slumber after being scratched by a thorny bramble.

PRINCE CHARMING

But like Sleeping Beauty, Princess Diana awoke, thanks to a kiss from a handsome prince… or a former one at least: Aquaman, King of Atlantis!

15

THE FLASH

JLA

LIFE IN ONE DAY

Wally West accomplishes more in a day than most people do in a week! powered by the Speed Force – an extra-dimensional energy field that fuels all super-speedsters – Wally's typical schedule includes housework, super-heroics, quality time with spouse Linda Park West, and some leisurely speed-reading.

WALLY WEST is the fastest man alive. As a boy, Wally idolized the second Flash, never dreaming that the Scarlet Speedster of Central City was secretly police scientist Barry Allen. After revealing his identity to the astonished Wally, Allen showed the youngster the laboratory where a shelf of chemicals had once been struck by lightning, dousing Barry in energized liquids and endowing him with super-speed! Incredibly, lightning struck twice in the same lab during Wally's visit, repeating the very same accident and creating another super-powered long-distance runner!

The Speed Force surrounds the Flash with a frictionless protective aura.

KID FLASH

When Wally became a pint-sized super-sprinter, the Flash immediately took him under his wing. As "Kid Flash," Wally sped alongside his uncle and mentor on many missions. After Barry Allen's untimely death, Wally reluctantly took up his crimson mantle and strove to follow in the Flash's impressive footsteps.

FLASH I

Jason "Jay" Garrick was himself hero to a young Barry Allen, who read and enjoyed the original human thunderbolt's exploits in the pages of comic books.

FLASH II

Bartholomew "Barry" Allen died racing to catch a reality-rending tachyon fired by the Earth-razing Anti-Monitor. Barry's grandson Bart inherited his connection to the Speed Force to become the young hero Impulse.

THE FLASH FAMILY

Wally West still looks to the eldest Flash for guidance. While technically a "senior citizen," the remarkably spry Jay Garrick can still run rings around his fleet-footed Flash family, including Wally, the Titans' Jesse Quick (herself daughter of late speedster Johnny Quick), and Young Justice's Impulse.

REAL NAME Wally West
OCCUPATION Adventurer
BASE Keystone City
HEIGHT 6 ft
WEIGHT 175 lb
EYES Green **HAIR** Red
FIRST APPEARANCE
THE FLASH #110
(December 1959–January 1960)

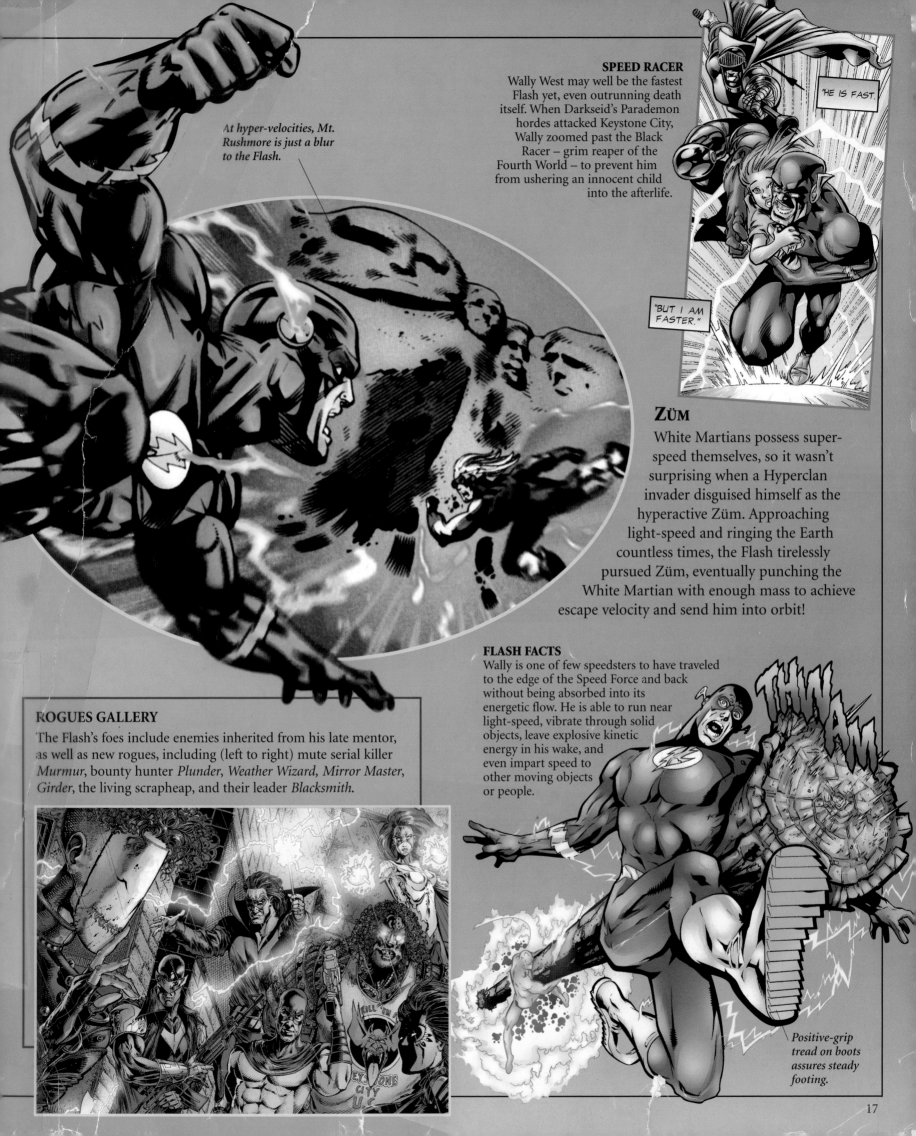

At hyper-velocities, Mt. Rushmore is just a blur to the Flash.

SPEED RACER

Wally West may well be the fastest Flash yet, even outrunning death itself. When Darkseid's Parademon hordes attacked Keystone City, Wally zoomed past the Black Racer – grim reaper of the Fourth World – to prevent him from ushering an innocent child into the afterlife.

"HE IS FAST."

"BUT I AM FASTER."

ZÜM

White Martians possess super-speed themselves, so it wasn't surprising when a Hyperclan invader disguised himself as the hyperactive Züm. Approaching light-speed and ringing the Earth countless times, the Flash tirelessly pursued Züm, eventually punching the White Martian with enough mass to achieve escape velocity and send him into orbit!

FLASH FACTS

Wally is one of few speedsters to have traveled to the edge of the Speed Force and back without being absorbed into its energetic flow. He is able to run near light-speed, vibrate through solid objects, leave explosive kinetic energy in his wake, and even impart speed to other moving objects or people.

THWAM

ROGUES GALLERY

The Flash's foes include enemies inherited from his late mentor, as well as new rogues, including (left to right) mute serial killer *Murmur*, bounty hunter *Plunder*, *Weather Wizard*, *Mirror Master*, *Girder*, the living scrapheap, and their leader *Blacksmith*.

Positive-grip tread on boots assures steady footing.

17

MARTIAN MANHUNTER

GREEN-SKINNED J'onn J'onzz is a lone survivor of the "Red Planet" Mars. Teleported to Earth by the brilliant Professor Saul Erdel, who was attempting to communicate between worlds, J'onn escaped a plague that wiped out the Martian population, including his family. Unable to return home, J'onn used his Martian shape-changing ability to take on the identity of a murdered police detective named John Jones. The Martian Manhunter became a hero secretly living among humans, who would otherwise have recoiled from his alien visage!

SHAPE-CHANGER

J'onn J'onzz's nervous system gives him control over his molecular structure. His silicon-based cells can alter to light-deflecting invisibility or, to more dramatic effect, enable him to change shape and assume any form for camouflage or disguise. Private detective John Jones is just one of many human identities the Manhunter maintains.

THE RED PLANET

Before their demise, the peaceful Green Martians devoted themselves to spiritual and mental development. Great cities once rose from the sandy soils of the Red Planet. In the ruins lie the graves of J'onn's beloved wife M'yri'ah and daughter K'hym.

SOLE SURVIVOR

On Earth, J'onn J'onzz reserves his natural Martian appearance for personal and private meditation, often reflecting on his lost life on Mars and H'ronmeer's Curse, the telepathic plague that left him the last of his kind. Having witnessed the fiery extinction of his own people, J'onn is determined to help safeguard Earth's population from a similarly horrific end.

MARTIAN MIND-READER

J'onn J'onzz's powers almost rival those of Superman. He can telepathically lay bare his foes' innermost thoughts. Telekinesis allows him to fly and gives him Martian Vision – focused blast-beams sufficient to perforate metal. He also wields great strength and incredible speed owing to superior Martian reflexes.

REAL NAME
J'onn J'onzz/John Jones
OCCUPATION Private Detective
BASE Denver, Colorado
HEIGHT 6 ft 7 in
WEIGHT 300 lb
EYES Red **HAIR** None
FIRST APPEARANCE
DETECTIVE COMICS #225
(November 1955)

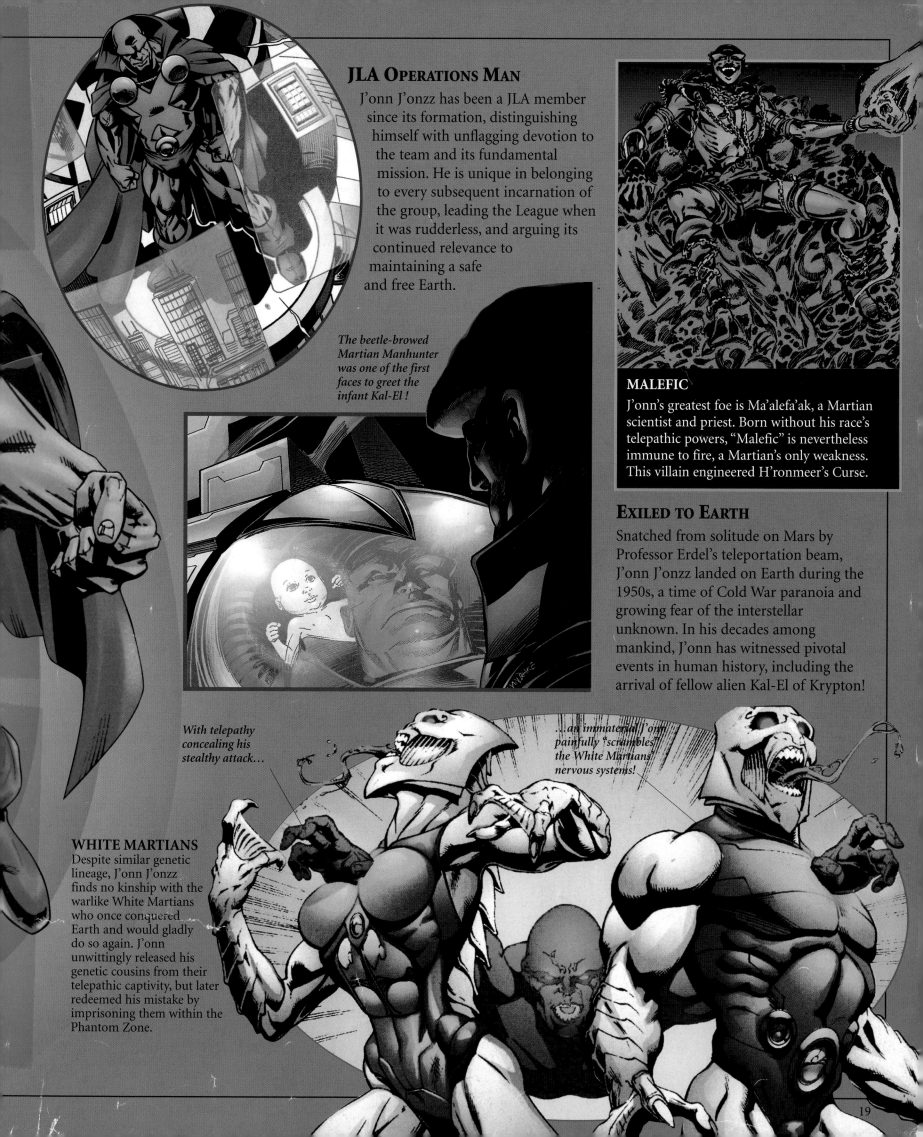

JLA OPERATIONS MAN

J'onn J'onzz has been a JLA member since its formation, distinguishing himself with unflagging devotion to the team and its fundamental mission. He is unique in belonging to every subsequent incarnation of the group, leading the League when it was rudderless, and arguing its continued relevance to maintaining a safe and free Earth.

The beetle-browed Martian Manhunter was one of the first faces to greet the infant Kal-El !

MALEFIC

J'onn's greatest foe is Ma'alefa'ak, a Martian scientist and priest. Born without his race's telepathic powers, "Malefic" is nevertheless immune to fire, a Martian's only weakness. This villain engineered H'ronmeer's Curse.

EXILED TO EARTH

Snatched from solitude on Mars by Professor Erdel's teleportation beam, J'onn J'onzz landed on Earth during the 1950s, a time of Cold War paranoia and growing fear of the interstellar unknown. In his decades among mankind, J'onn has witnessed pivotal events in human history, including the arrival of fellow alien Kal-El of Krypton!

With telepathy concealing his stealthy attack…

…an immaterial J'onn painfully "scrambles" the White Martians' nervous systems!

WHITE MARTIANS

Despite similar genetic lineage, J'onn J'onzz finds no kinship with the warlike White Martians who once conquered Earth and would gladly do so again. J'onn unwittingly released his genetic cousins from their telepathic captivity, but later redeemed his mistake by imprisoning them within the Phantom Zone.

GREEN LANTERN

JLA

THE OAN POWER RING is the most formidable armament ever devised. Created by the immortal Guardians of the Universe, this will-powered weapon is the last of its kind. It is now worn by Kyle Rayner, inheritor of the great legacy of the Green Lantern Corps. 3,600 beings once patrolled as many space sectors in the service of the Guardians. Kyle is all that remains. He succeeded Hal Jordan, whose quest for the emerald energies to resurrect his decimated home town of Coast City drove him mad and led to the destruction of both the Corps and its Guardian masters. Yet one Guardian survived, journeying to Earth and bequeathing the sole remaining power ring to Kyle Rayner, the last Green Lantern!

FREELANCE ARTIST

Somehow, Kyle Rayner finds time to be Green Lantern and work as a freelance artist! Kyle's vivid imagination fuels the incredible solid-light manifestations willed into existence with his power ring. In civilian life, he contributes the popular "City Dwellers" cartoon strip to the New York-based *Feast* magazine. His occasional caricatures of fellow JLA teammates are merely for his own personal pleasure.

GANTHET

The Guardians of the Universe surrendered their own immortal life essences to create one final power ring. Only Ganthet remained to find a worthy candidate for the ring. He now watches over the young Guardians restored to life by Kyle Rayner.

JADE

Kyle's girlfriend, Jennie-Lynn Hayden is the daughter of Alan Scott – Earth's first Green Lantern – and the villainess Thorn. Jen once possessed emerald energies as the green-skinned heroine Jade. Though she lost those powers, Jade maintains some plant-based abilities, and fights alongside Kyle with a replicated power ring forged just for her.

OUT OF POWER

Kyle occasionally replenishes his ring with a lantern-shaped Oan power battery, just like the previous Corps members. However, Kyle recently reconfigured his ring so that it always maintains a reserve charge.

FATALITY

Kyle's most determined foe is the alien warrior Yrra Cynril, a.k.a. Fatality. Yrra cut a vengeful swath across the universe, murdering any former Green Lantern she found in revenge for the accidental destruction of her home planet, Xanshi, by Earth-born GL John Stewart. Fatality is a mistress of many weapons, and now boasts two bionic arms after her original limbs were lost in battle with Kyle Rayner.

BEWARE HIS POWER!

In its heyday, the Green Lantern Corps employed an armada of alien agents, each one utterly devoid of fear. Their incredible power rings, coveted across the cosmos, were nevertheless rendered impotent by the color yellow, an inherent weakness in their construction. Kyle Rayner's ring was unique, cleansed of the yellow impurity and able to replicate itself if necessary. When combined with Kyle's willpower and imagination, this last ring can accomplish virtually anything.

The Green Lantern insignia is recognized throughout the universe as a badge of justice and honor.

IT'S THE ULTIMATE EXECUTIVE TOY, MAN! A HEAD THAT DRINKS THE OCEAN! GIMME FIVE MINUTES TO DUMP THESE GUYS SOMEWHERE WARM.

MAGEDDON

For millennia, the Ultimate Warbringer watched the universe, particularly the exploits of the Green Lanterns. When the Mageddon warhead targeted Earth, the Primordial Annihilator first moved to neutralize Kyle Rayner, employing Prometheus and the Red Dart to separate the Green Lantern from his will-powered bauble!

ALAN SCOTT
Earth's first Green Lantern carved his ring and battery of power from the Starheart, a green-glowing meteor within which the Guardians gathered the random magicks of the universe.

HAL JORDAN
Earthman Hal Jordan was perhaps the Corps' most distinguished agent, patrolling Space Sector 2814 with fearlessness and devotion. Though Hal ultimately destroyed the Corps, he redeems himself now as the otherworldly Spectre.

A NEW LOOK

Kyle abandoned his original Green Lantern costume when he became the all-knowing Ion. He nearly used his great might to rewrite every wrong by revising history itself – Hal Jordan's fatal mistake – but relinquished his all-powerful abilities to resurrect the Guardians. To show the changes in his life and perspective, Kyle adopted a dynamic new costume for the Emerald Warrior.

REAL NAME	Kyle Rayner
OCCUPATION	Freelance Artist
BASE	New York City
HEIGHT	5 ft 11 in
WEIGHT	175 lb
EYES Dark Green	**HAIR** Black

FIRST APPEARANCE
GREEN LANTERN
(3rd series) #48
(January 1994)

While Kyle's ring maintains an emergency reserve of power, it still requires charging when "full power" is necessary.

PLASTIC MAN

PLIABLE PRANKSTER Eel O'Brian may have started out on the wrong side of the tracks, but he is working very hard to redeem his past indiscretions. Decades ago, O'Brian was a lowlife gangster with a complete disregard for the law. That all changed after a freak accident that rendered O'Brian decidedly more *impressionable*. Made over as a stretchable super hero, O'Brian became Plastic Man, a costumed champion active since World War II. Still springy and supple some 60 years later, Plas continues his high-tensile hijinks as a permanent member of the JLA!

HE GOT EEL!

BENDY HERO

THIS IS NASTYYYYY!

As a result of his chemical metamorphosis, Plas has near-complete control of his body's elasticity. He can elongate or compress himself into virtually any shape. He can also mimic people, animals, or objects to disguise himself. Yet, after six decades of pliant properties, he still can't readily alter his physical color.

ORIGINAL SKIN

In 1941, Eel O'Brian attempted to rob the Crawford Chemical Works and was shot by a security guard. He stumbled into a vat of acid, and caustic solvents slopped into his wounds. O'Brian escaped capture and found his way to the Rest-Haven monastic retreat. There he discovered that the acids had made his body incredibly malleable. And with the monks influence, O'Brian molded himself into a heroic Plastic Man!

REAL NAME Eel O'Brian
OCCUPATION Crime Fighter
BASE New York City
HEIGHT 6 ft 1 in
WEIGHT 178 lb
EYES Brown **HAIR** Black
FIRST APPEARANCE POLICE COMICS #1 (August 1941)

BUGGED OUT

Although limited to crimson hues, Plastic Man's monochromatic morphings did come in handy during the Justice League's quarrel with the Queen Bee. Unable to see the color red, the Queen barely registered Plastic Man's attack as a giant can of insecticide!

NO ANGEL

Batman is aware of Plastic Man's ignoble past. However, the Dark Knight nominated Plas for League membership after successfully teaming up with him on several cases.

STRETCHABLE SLEUTH

After serving both the wartime All-Star Squadron and Freedom Fighters with distinction, Plas was employed by the F.B.I. and then its sister agency the National Bureau of Investigations. As an N.B.I. operative, Plas partnered agent Woozy Winks. Together, this fun-loving, daring duo saved the world from such villains as the Dart, Even Steven, and the Brotherhood of the Savage Caribou. Despite reports to the contrary, Plas never tackled the terrorist Bane. But when he does, watch out!

"Groovy Goggles" protect Plastic Man's identity and give him a unique perspective on super-heroics.

TRICKSTER GOD

The Injustice Gang's Circe once mistook Plas for Dionysos, the form-changing Greek god of wine and debauchery. Although Plas is definitely mortal in tastes and appetites, he does resemble tricksters of myth in his penchant for tormenting foes with his plastic fantastic antics.

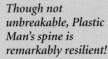

Though not unbreakable, Plastic Man's spine is remarkably resilient!

COMIC RELIEF

Plas may not be the most outwardly serious of super heroes, but he is committed to the Justice League. Plastic Man's mercurial personality underscores his ability to think on his feet and adapt to any situation. While his incessant joking occasionally wears on his JLA teammates, Plas provides welcome comic relief, whether morphing into a zany and zaftig Amazon (left) or popping his eyes out in mock despair to break the tension during a potential cosmic calamity.

THE BIG SQUEEZE

White Martians may be able to molecularly metamorphose their forms into any hideous beasts, but these alien attackers lack Plastic Man's flamboyant flair for the dramatic. Proving himself more snake than "Eel," a serpentine Plas squeezed one hapless Martian into surrendering.

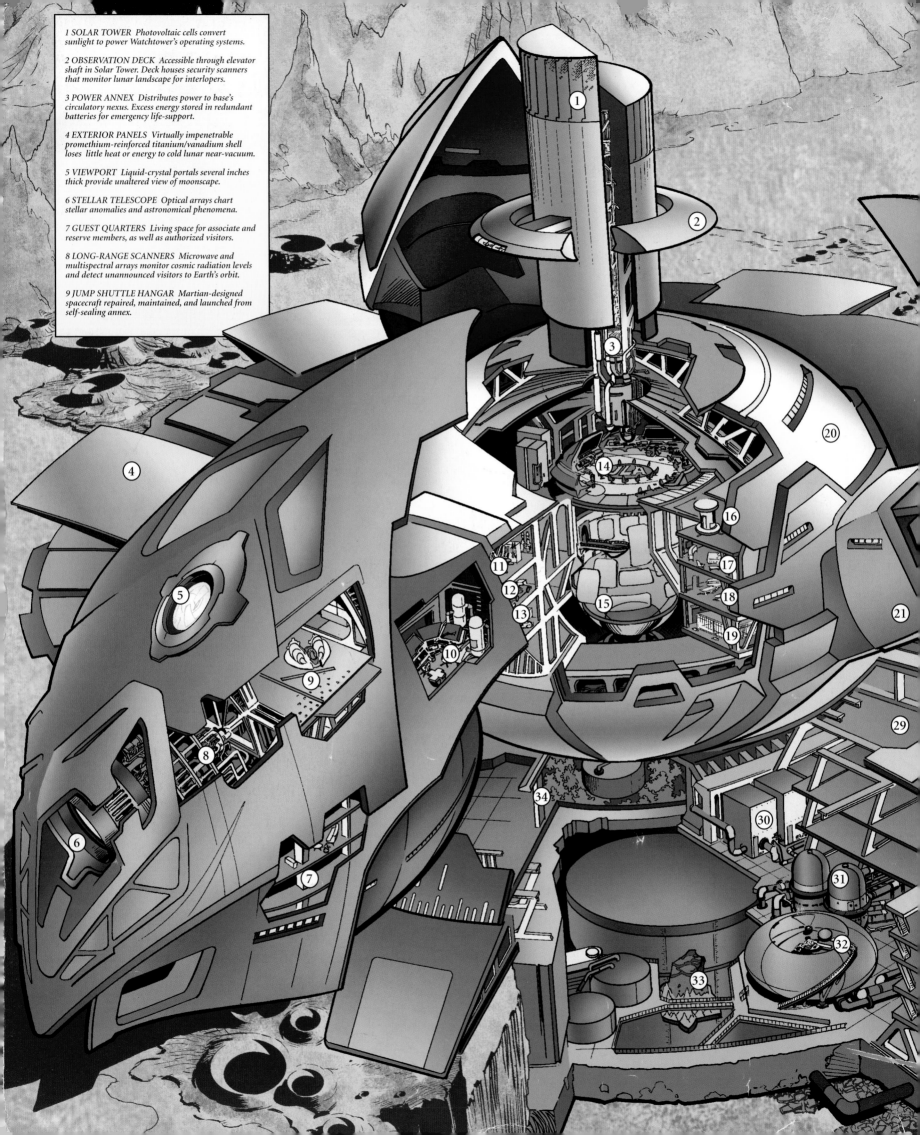

1 SOLAR TOWER Photovoltaic cells convert sunlight to power Watchtower's operating systems.

2 OBSERVATION DECK Accessible through elevator shaft in Solar Tower. Deck houses security scanners that monitor lunar landscape for interlopers.

3 POWER ANNEX Distributes power to base's circulatory nexus. Excess energy stored in redundant batteries for emergency life-support.

4 EXTERIOR PANELS Virtually impenetrable promethium-reinforced titanium/vanadium shell loses little heat or energy to cold lunar near-vacuum.

5 VIEWPORT Liquid-crystal portals several inches thick provide unaltered view of moonscape.

6 STELLAR TELESCOPE Optical arrays chart stellar anomalies and astronomical phenomena.

7 GUEST QUARTERS Living space for associate and reserve members, as well as authorized visitors.

8 LONG-RANGE SCANNERS Microwave and multispectral arrays monitor cosmic radiation levels and detect unannounced visitors to Earth's orbit.

9 JUMP SHUTTLE HANGAR Martian-designed spacecraft repaired, maintained, and launched from self-sealing annex.

THE WATCHTOWER

JLA

NESTLED AMID THE CRATERED lunar surface is the Justice League's latest and most advanced HQ. The JLA first convened in the "Secret Sanctuary," a mountain cavern near Happy Harbor, Rhode Island. Soon, security concerns forced the team to relocate to a satellite orbiting 22,300 miles above the Earth. The League later made its home in "The Bunker," an armory buried beneath an abandoned factory in Detroit, Michigan. More recent incarnations of the team were based in unassuming embassies, including New York City, Paris, and even Antarctic sites. These days, the JLA holds court in the Watchtower, a fortress erected in the Moon's *Mare Serenitatis* ("The Sea of Serenity").

10 STEEL'S WORKSHOP High-tech foundry and lab includes secondary surveillance controls.

11 ARMORY Secure vault for "last resort" weapons and other technological countermeasures.

12 TROPHY ROOM Contains mementos – some authentic, others facsimiles – of JLA adventures.

13 ADDITIONAL STORAGE Spare parts, supplies, and items from previous headquarters kept here.

14 HALL OF JUSTICE The JLA's meeting chamber.

15 MONITOR WOMB Interactive computer systems monitor global mass media footage and feed "real-time" holographic displays around floating suspensor chair. League member on monitor duty assesses potential "trouble-alerts."

16 TELEPORT TUBE Sender/receiver unit utilizes "ambient matter" to teleport organic beings.

WATCHTOWER II
This is the second Watchtower, rebuilt and redesigned after the Injustice Gang razed the original structure during the onset of World War III.

17 LIVING QUARTERS Personalized suites for all active members.

18 GALLEY Kitchen and dining area provides Earthly and extraterrestrial cuisine and is stocked with dietary requirements of each League member.

19 BULK TELEPORTER Larger teleport unit transmits only inorganic matter, ferrying supplies and equipment to and from the Watchtower.

20 CENTRAL HUB An external casing surrounds the shielded hub core with its meeting and living areas protected by individual self-sealing airlocks.

21 SPOKE TERMINUS Each of the Watchtower's three "spoke" wings can be hermetically isolated from the hub, or jettisoned using minimal ion-propulsion units to break lunar orbit during emergency egresses.

22 GYMNASIUM Includes training areas and virtual-reality battle environments.

23 POOL Low-saline pool provides exercise and relaxation for League members.

24 ARBORETUM Endangered species of flora and fauna find safe haven in segregated micro-ecosystems.

25 FLIGHT BRIDGE Contains navigational controls and life-support systems.

26 JLA-1 Larger multiseat sublight shuttle takes off and lands like traditional aircraft.

27 ENTRY PORT Provides access for incoming ships to disembark in primary hangar.

28 SEISMIC SENSORS Early warning system to detect "moonquakes" in lunar substrata.

29 PRIMARY HANGAR Launch platform and berthing for JLA-1.

30 CO_2 SCRUBBERS Sweep internal air systems for carbon dioxide, removing pathogens before feeding gases to hydroponic forest.

31 HYDROGEN GENERATOR PODS Back-up power systems split hydrogen atoms from mined water for fusion in reactors. Oxygen by-product released into ventilation ducts.

32 DEEP-BORE ICE MINER Extracts ice buried beneath lunar soil, cleaning and purifying resulting H_2O for use throughout base.

33 DEEP WATER TANK Stores fresh water produced by deep-bore ice miner in large aquifer. Adjacent artificial "hot spring" doubles as sauna.

34 HYDROPONIC FOREST Photosynthesis-reliant plants convert CO_2 into oxygen, providing base with recyclable air supply.

INSIDE THE WATCHTOWER

JLA

WHILE SPECTACULAR FROM THE OUTSIDE, the interior of the JLA Watchtower is no less impressive. Built and maintained by the World's Greatest Super Heroes, their near-impregnable lunar citadel features an amalgam of fantastic technologies: Kryptonian, Martian, and New Genesian, to name but a few. This perimeter fortress is home away from home for many of the League members, while serving as primary staging ground for guarding against threats both alien and terrestrial. As such, the Watchtower includes the most advanced monitoring systems and transport media to ensure the JLA is always one step ahead of Earthly emergencies… even from a headquarters as far as 252,950 miles away!

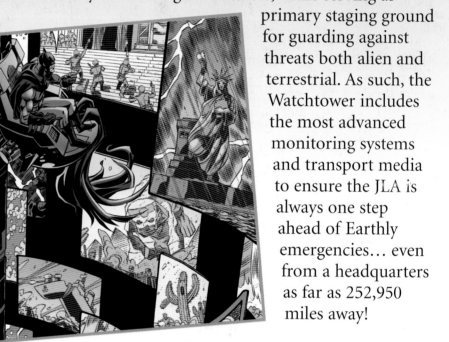

Like its namesake in Arthurian legend, the Round Table symbolizes unity, an unbroken circle that stresses equality over precedence.

ROUND TABLE AND MONITOR WOMB

At the center of the Hall of Justice, the Watchtower's meeting room, stands the Round Table. Here the team meets to strategize and share information. Directly beneath the Hall of Justice lies the Monitor Womb (right), the League's eyes and ears. Inside this surveillance hub, interactive computer systems monitor global media broadcasts for "Trouble-Alerts," displaying crises upon holographic displays.

JUMP SHUTTLE

Since only a few JLA members can fly of their own accord — let alone travel through space — the team utilizes a small squadron of Jump Shuttles patterned along Martian designs and powered by sound-propelled, cold-fusion reactors. Smaller shuttles are used for solo flights, while larger ships have room to ferry the whole team across interstellar voids.

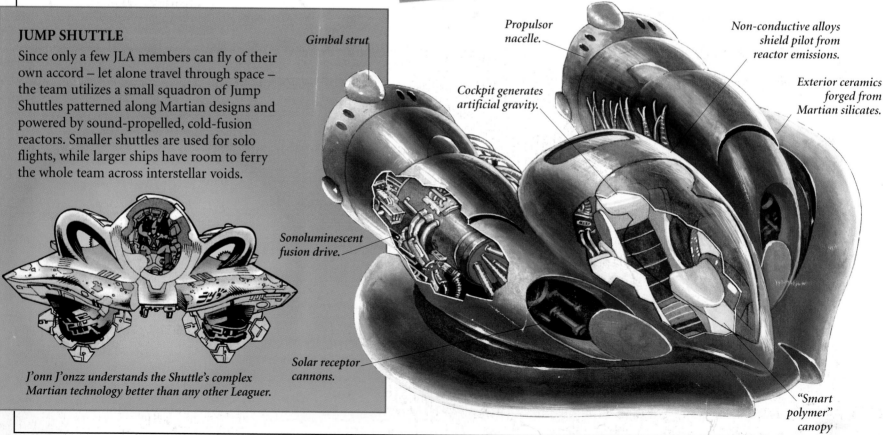

Gimbal strut

Propulsor nacelle.

Cockpit generates artificial gravity.

Non-conductive alloys shield pilot from reactor emissions.

Exterior ceramics forged from Martian silicates.

Sonoluminescent fusion drive.

Solar receptor cannons.

"Smart polymer" canopy

J'onn J'onzz understands the Shuttle's complex Martian technology better than any other Leaguer.

SECURITY MEASURES

The Justice League has taken great pains to make the Watchtower self-sufficient and secure from attack. Hydroponic forests fed by Aquaman's deep water tanks create a living biosphere within the facility, replenishing oxygen. Each wing of the Watchtower also includes its own independently sealing airlock to prevent decompression or fire, or to contain attackers undeterred by the internal battery of security snares, paralysis pits, and electromagnetic cages.

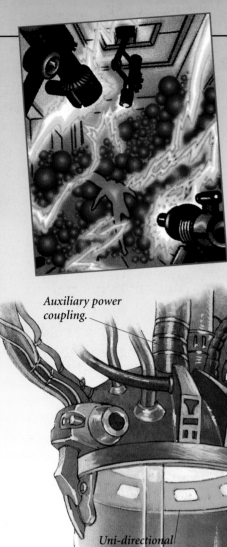

Super-escape artist Mr. Miracle evades the Watchtower security snares!

Auxiliary power coupling.

Security sensors in tube trap all unauthorized teleporters in immaterial energy flux.

Uni-directional teleport gateway.

Thanagarian crystalline containment tube.

Virtual display monitors and calibrates all receiver modules.

PROMETHEUS BREAK-IN

Bio-scanners arrayed throughout the Watchtower register the DNA signatures of League members and associate heroes. Prometheus figured as much. That's why the hero-killer sneaked into the Watchtower during a press junket when the scanners expected unknown visitors! Prometheus then downloaded the Watchtower blueprints into his brain before setting fire to the oxygen-recycling hydroponic forest!

TELEPORTERS

Since first occupying a space-based headquarters – initially a satellite in geosynchronous orbit 22,300 miles above the Earth – the JLA has relied on teleporting science. The League's current teleport tube technology comes from the planet Thanagar, once home to the reincarnated Hawkman. "Ambient Matter" creates linkages from sender tubes to identical receiver modules, literally folding space to create stabilized wormholes between two distant points.

Teleport tube control kiosk.

Ambient matter in stationary phase-shift.

BULK TELEPORTER

The team also makes much use of a larger bulk teleporter to bring equipment and supplies to their lunar retreat. The bulk teleporter does not require a receiver module. On one occasion, this allowed the League to transport the rampaging, non-biological General out of the Watchtower and into deep space!

Quarantine step-pads sterilize all transmissions

ALLIES OF THE LEAGUE

JLA

ONCE A JUSTICE LEAGUER, always a Justice Leaguer. While the JLA roster has waxed and waned over the years – with nearly 100 super heroes listed on the official roll call during its various incarnations – almost every previous member remains ready to answer the call in the event of a crisis. Each defender brings his or her own unique contribution to the League. When scientific savvy is required, Steel or The Atom is the first to be consulted. And the Justice League knows that *two* Green Arrows are better than one. Oracle provides earthbound information with digital dispatch, while Zauriel is a divine messenger warning of evils springing forth from the afterlife. The Huntress, Firestorm, Hourman, and Aztek have all fought nobly, though only three survived to tell the tale. The formidable Orion and Big Barda are merely a Boom Tube away from their former teammates. And while the Justice Society of America reflects the JLA's history, The Titans and Young Justice may well be the Justice League's *future*. These stalwart heroes and heroines are friends indeed when the JLA is in need of super-powered reinforcements.

I'VE GOT HIM, SUPERMAN!

HAMMER ON MAXIMUM!

UURRNNNNN

STEEL

JLA

JOHN HENRY IRONS never expected to become a hero. But when the brilliant engineer discovered that his employer – the military industrial complex AmerTek – had misused the weapons he designed, Irons sabotaged his own work. Changing his life meant changing his career, and John Henry became a construction worker plying the high steel of Metropolis. A fall from the tall support struts of a skyscraper would have spelled certain death for Irons if not for Superman's timely intervention. John Henry was so inspired in meeting the Man of Steel that he forged a suit of armor to honor him. As Steel, Irons now battles evil as one of Superman's closest friends and allies.

I MADE A BET WITH MYSELF: I BET I COULD FIX IT BEFORE SUNSET.

GENERAL NUISANCE!

Joining the JLA during its most recent membership drive, Steel's tenure with the team was short. He served with distinction during the Mageddon crisis, barely survived the maw of the General, and helped adapt an Amazonian Purple "Healing" Ray to temporarily energize Earth's populace with metahuman powers.

PLUGGED IN

Superman himself nominated the armor-clad Steel for League induction, realizing that the team lacked practical scientific expertise. After taking his oath of membership, John Henry established a high-tech workshop in the Watchtower. One of his first tasks was to upgrade the headquarters' security systems, wiring the web of non-lethal deterrents to controls within the workshop. The efficiency-minded engineer configured his own armor systems to allow access to the entire Watchtower security grid.

SOMETHING'S NOT RIGHT. I'M SORRY, STEEL, I CAN'T BE ANY MORE SPECIFIC. IT'S LIKE SOMEONE'S IN HERE WITH ME...

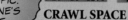

NNGH.

NNF

ONE STEP AT A TIME

CRAWL SPACE

When Triumph betrayed the JLA, Steel was forced to shed his armor and retreat into the Watchtower's access tunnels. But the tables were turned when Steel plugged himself into the citadel's security systems, literally *wearing* the building as unassailable replacement armor!

MASTER FORGER

Steel's workshop houses a foundry for building and maintaining his armor. Although now scaled back to "Associate" membership, John Henry occasionally visits this lunar laboratory to tinker with New Genesis technology left by Orion and Barda.

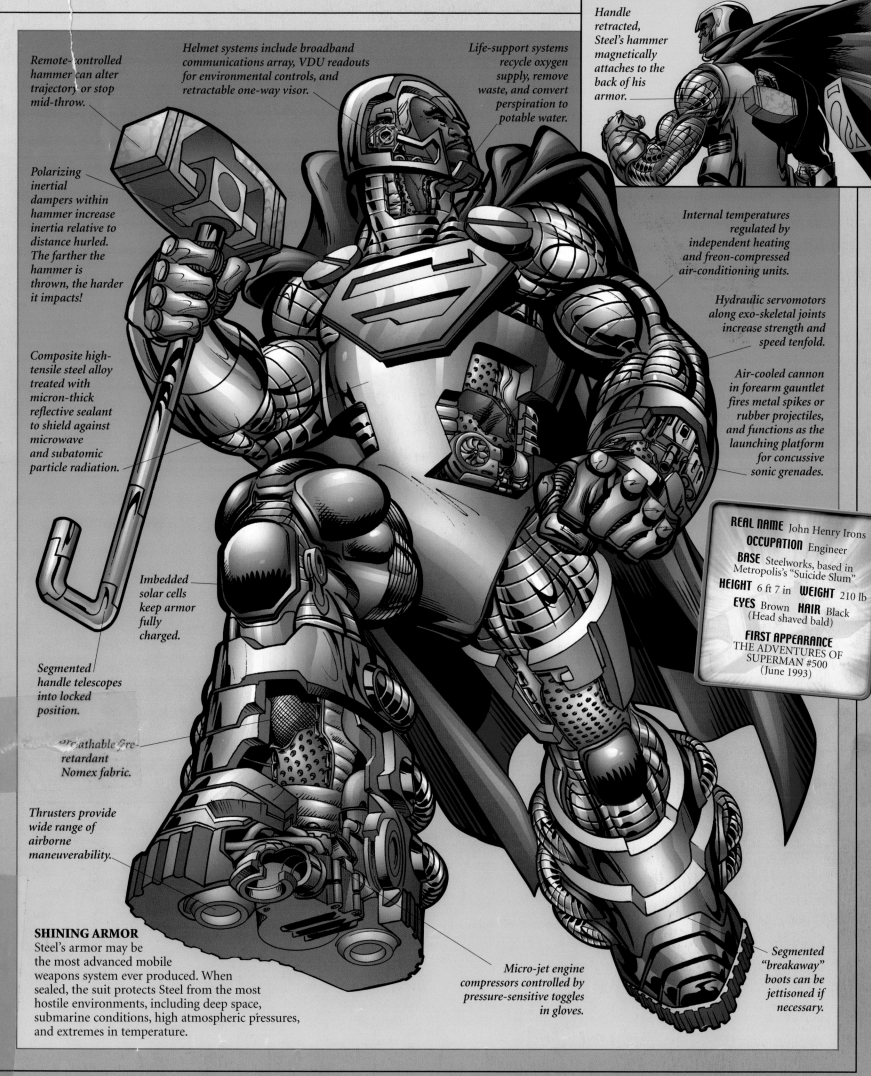

Remote-controlled hammer can alter trajectory or stop mid-throw.

Helmet systems include broadband communications array, VDU readouts for environmental controls, and retractable one-way visor.

Life-support systems recycle oxygen supply, remove waste, and convert perspiration to potable water.

Handle retracted, Steel's hammer magnetically attaches to the back of his armor.

Polarizing inertial dampers within hammer increase inertia relative to distance hurled. The farther the hammer is thrown, the harder it impacts!

Composite high-tensile steel alloy treated with micron-thick reflective sealant to shield against microwave and subatomic particle radiation.

Internal temperatures regulated by independent heating and freon-compressed air-conditioning units.

Hydraulic servomotors along exo-skeletal joints increase strength and speed tenfold.

Air-cooled cannon in forearm gauntlet fires metal spikes or rubber projectiles, and functions as the launching platform for concussive sonic grenades.

Imbedded solar cells keep armor fully charged.

Segmented handle telescopes into locked position.

Breathable fire-retardant Nomex fabric.

Thrusters provide wide range of airborne maneuverability.

SHINING ARMOR
Steel's armor may be the most advanced mobile weapons system ever produced. When sealed, the suit protects Steel from the most hostile environments, including deep space, submarine conditions, high atmospheric pressures, and extremes in temperature.

Micro-jet engine compressors controlled by pressure-sensitive toggles in gloves.

Segmented "breakaway" boots can be jettisoned if necessary.

REAL NAME John Henry Irons
OCCUPATION Engineer
BASE Steelworks, based in Metropolis's "Suicide Slum"
HEIGHT 6 ft 7 in **WEIGHT** 210 lb
EYES Brown **HAIR** Black (Head shaved bald)
FIRST APPEARANCE
THE ADVENTURES OF SUPERMAN #500 (June 1993)

GREEN ARROW

Two battling bowmen have sat at the Justice League round table, the first and only father-and-son members of the terrific team. While marooned on Starfish Island, playboy Oliver Queen taught himself archery to survive, later wielding his bow as Green Arrow, a modern-day Robin Hood. He joined the fledgling JLA as its sixth official member. Years later, Queen's son Connor Hawke became an Emerald Archer and gained League membership. Both are currently JLA Reservists, ready to nock arrows should the need arise.

REAL NAME	Oliver Queen
OCCUPATION	Vigilante
BASE	Star City
HEIGHT	5 ft 11 in
WEIGHT	185 lb
EYES Green	**HAIR** Blond

FIRST APPEARANCE
MORE FUN COMICS #73
(November 1941)

OLIVER QUEEN

Through all his romantic adventures, Oliver Queen's one true love is Dinah Lance, the Black Canary. The two began a passionate relationship while members of the League's original lineup. Despite drifting apart, they still share a deep and abiding affection for each other.

RUFFLED FEATHERS
The liberal-minded Green Arrow frequently engaged his fellow members in ideological debates concerning the Justice League's proper role in world affairs. In particular, he clashed with the more conservative Hawkman. Although trusted allies, neither would ever admit to liking the other.

RETURNED FROM THE DEAD
Not long ago, Oliver Queen sacrificed his own life to stop a bio-terrorist attack on Metropolis. Reports of his death, however, became greatly exaggerated when Hal Jordan – brandishing the emerald energies of the all-powerful Parallax – restored Ollie to life, much to his former teammates' joy.

AMAZING ARROWS

To find food on Starfish Island, Oliver Queen fashioned trick arrows to net fish and pluck coconuts from trees. He adapted these designs and many more as Green Arrow, adding Acetylene, Acid, Bola, Grappling Hook, Cryonic, Tear Gas, and other ingenious arrows to his quiver. The Boxing Glove Arrow (seen here) was one of his most effective.

AAAH!

WHUMP!

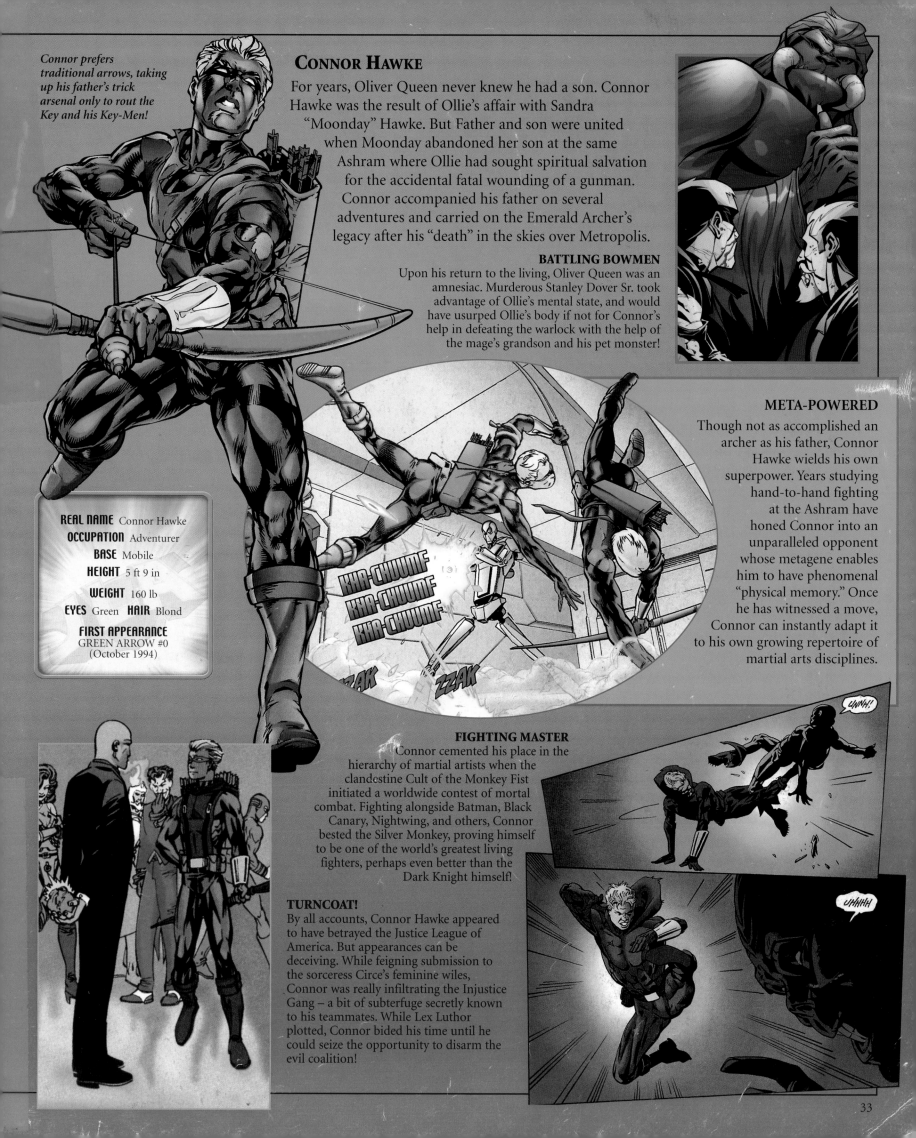

Connor prefers traditional arrows, taking up his father's trick arsenal only to rout the Key and his Key-Men!

CONNOR HAWKE

For years, Oliver Queen never knew he had a son. Connor Hawke was the result of Ollie's affair with Sandra "Moonday" Hawke. But Father and son were united when Moonday abandoned her son at the same Ashram where Ollie had sought spiritual salvation for the accidental fatal wounding of a gunman. Connor accompanied his father on several adventures and carried on the Emerald Archer's legacy after his "death" in the skies over Metropolis.

BATTLING BOWMEN

Upon his return to the living, Oliver Queen was an amnesiac. Murderous Stanley Dover Sr. took advantage of Ollie's mental state, and would have usurped Ollie's body if not for Connor's help in defeating the warlock with the help of the mage's grandson and his pet monster!

META-POWERED

Though not as accomplished an archer as his father, Connor Hawke wields his own superpower. Years studying hand-to-hand fighting at the Ashram have honed Connor into an unparalleled opponent whose metagene enables him to have phenomenal "physical memory." Once he has witnessed a move, Connor can instantly adapt it to his own growing repertoire of martial arts disciplines.

REAL NAME Connor Hawke
OCCUPATION Adventurer
BASE Mobile
HEIGHT 5 ft 9 in
WEIGHT 160 lb
EYES Green **HAIR** Blond
FIRST APPEARANCE GREEN ARROW #0 (October 1994)

FIGHTING MASTER

Connor cemented his place in the hierarchy of martial artists when the clandestine Cult of the Monkey Fist initiated a worldwide contest of mortal combat. Fighting alongside Batman, Black Canary, Nightwing, and others, Connor bested the Silver Monkey, proving himself to be one of the world's greatest living fighters, perhaps even better than the Dark Knight himself!

TURNCOAT!

By all accounts, Connor Hawke appeared to have betrayed the Justice League of America. But appearances can be deceiving. While feigning submission to the sorceress Circe's feminine wiles, Connor was really infiltrating the Injustice Gang – a bit of subterfuge secretly known to his teammates. While Lex Luthor plotted, Connor bided his time until he could seize the opportunity to disarm the evil coalition!

Oracle

BARBARA GORDON was determined to fight crime. Inspired by Gotham City's Dark Knight vigilante, the adopted daughter of former G.C.P.D. Commissioner James Gordon took up her own cloak and cowl as Batgirl. Barbara soon became Batman's ally. Unfortunately, she also gained the enmity of his Rogues Gallery. The Caped Crusader's worst foe – The Joker – shot and paralyzed Barbara in her own home. Her spirit unbroken, Barbara became the all-seeing Oracle, using her unparalleled computer savvy to continue upholding justice.

REAL NAME	Barbara Gordon
OCCUPATION	Information Broker
BASE	Gotham City
HEIGHT	5 ft 6 in
WEIGHT	126 lb
EYES Green	**HAIR** Red
FIRST APPEARANCE	DETECTIVE COMICS #359 (January 1967)

DIGITAL DOMAIN

As a JLA "Associate," Oracle has never visited the Watchtower. She operates out of her self-sufficient and secure headquarters in the historic Gotham City Clocktower. There she maintains six Yale super-computers storing digital databases on every known metahuman crime or criminal.

PROMETHEUS ATTACKS!

Oracle's state-of-the-art Clocktower facility includes its own power source and a variety of non-lethal deterrents to repel intruders, including motion detectors, video surveillance, regurgitant gas aerosols, and various electrified thresholds. Despite these measures, the hero-hunter Prometheus laid siege to the Clocktower and attacked Oracle on her home turf!

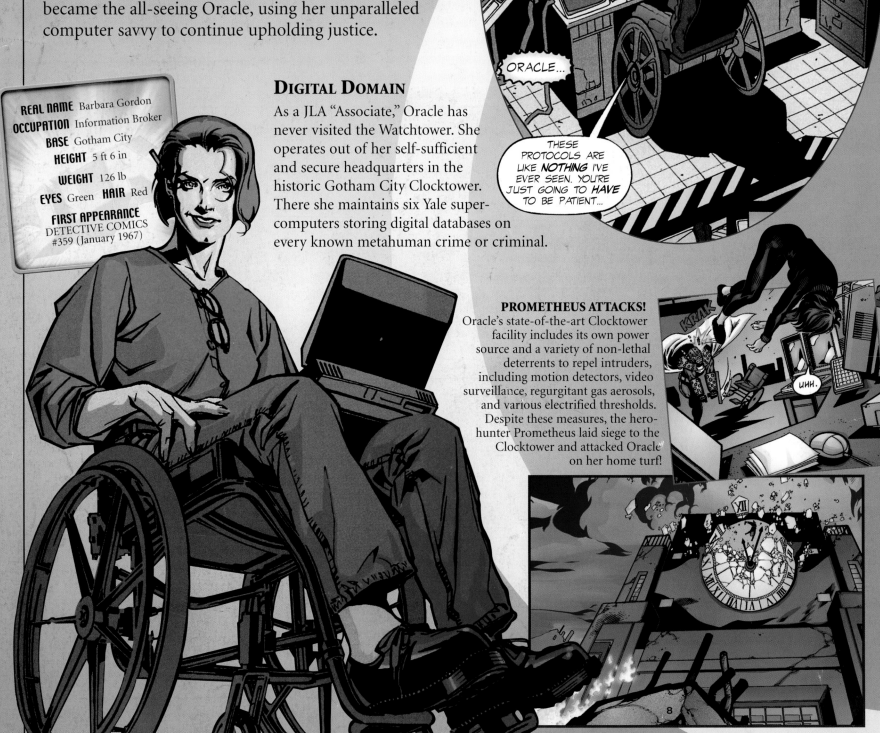

THE MASK OF ORACLE

Though most Justice League members know the truth behind the teammate designated "Data Central," Barbara Gordon continues to cloak her identity with a holographic display based on the funerary mask of the Trojan oracle Cassandra. Gifted with prophecy by the Greek god Apollo, Cassandra's warnings were fated to go unheeded. Fortunately, Barbara Gordon's criminal profiles and assessments are highly regarded in the JLA. Oracle's battlefield analyses – enabled via J'onn J'onzz's telepathic links – have often helped the JLA win the day.

Strategically placed hologram generators allow the all-seeing Oracle a pixilated presence throughout the JLA Watchtower.

BLACK CANARY

Dinah Laurel Lance has the distinction of being the JLA's very first female member and one of the team's founding five heroes. A second-generation costumed adventurer, Dinah is the daughter of the Black Canary, a blonde-bombshell heroine of the Justice Society. Donning her mother's fishnets and leather, Dinah's latter-day Canary helped to defeat the invading Appellaxian aliens and create a coalition of the World's Greatest Super Heroes. She has since served courageously with nearly every incarnation of the team.

SONIC SCREAM

Dinah is a master judo practitioner like her mother. But unlike the original Black Canary, Dinah was born with a metagene and her own unique superpower, an ear-splitting hypersonic "Canary Cry." A traumatic physical assault robbed Dinah of this meta-ability for some time, although a dip in Rā's al Ghūl's restorative "Lazarus Pit" healed her damaged vocal chords and allowed the Canary to sing her destructive song anew.

BIRDS OF PREY

While remaining a "Reserve" member of the JLA, Black Canary also belongs to the new Justice Society. But as a solo heroine, she serves as Oracle's primary field operative and troubleshooter. This paid position is enabled through Oracle's electronic seizure of criminals' ill-gotten funds. Since beginning their crime-busting alliance, the two heroines have become fast friends.

ASSOCIATE DEGREE

After serving the JLA with distinction for many years, the Mighty Mite is now an "Associate" team member. In addition to providing scientific expertise, the Atom frequently volunteers for monitor duty. Otherwise, Ray Palmer remains a physics professor at the prestigious Ivy University. There the super hero keeps office hours in a miniaturized laboratory on his desktop.

THE ATOM

THE FALLEN FRAGMENT of a white dwarf star turned physicist Ray Palmer into a Tiny Titan! Palmer had previously experimented with reducing matter, although his samples all exploded from molecular instability. The white dwarf fragment helped forestall that catastrophic end, especially after Palmer shrunk himself in order to rescue young spelunkers trapped in a cave-in. When combined with ultraviolet light, mineral-laden cave water, and his own unique physiology, Palmer's white dwarf enabled him to save the day. Later, upon donning his own specialized costume to control the changes in his size and weight, Ray Palmer adapted this miraculous innovation to battle crime as the Atom!

DIMINUTIVE DOCTOR

Although he holds advanced degrees in particle and quantum physics, Ray Palmer is the world's foremost authority on micro-medicine. Able to reduce his six-foot frame past the size of cellular nuclei and into the invisible realm of complex DNA chains, the Atom can enter a patient's body and perform life-saving operations way beyond the scope of normal surgery.

BRAINSCAPE

At 2,500 angstroms (.00000025 meters), the Atom surveys a microscopic city growing out of a child's brain like some malignant cancer. To prevent the spread of infection in this unique surgical field, the Tiny Titan wears sanitized breather gear.

PARASITIC INFECTION

The Atom expected a routine tumor excision. But when the Mighty Mite entered the cerebellum of a desperately ill young boy, he discovered a microscopic civilization. In their tumor-like city of 30 million inhabitants, these bacteria-beings strip-mined the boy's gray matter for raw dendrite material to fuel their microbial metropolis!

The JLA went on a microscopic mission to save the boy's life, but found their powers diminished at subatomic size!

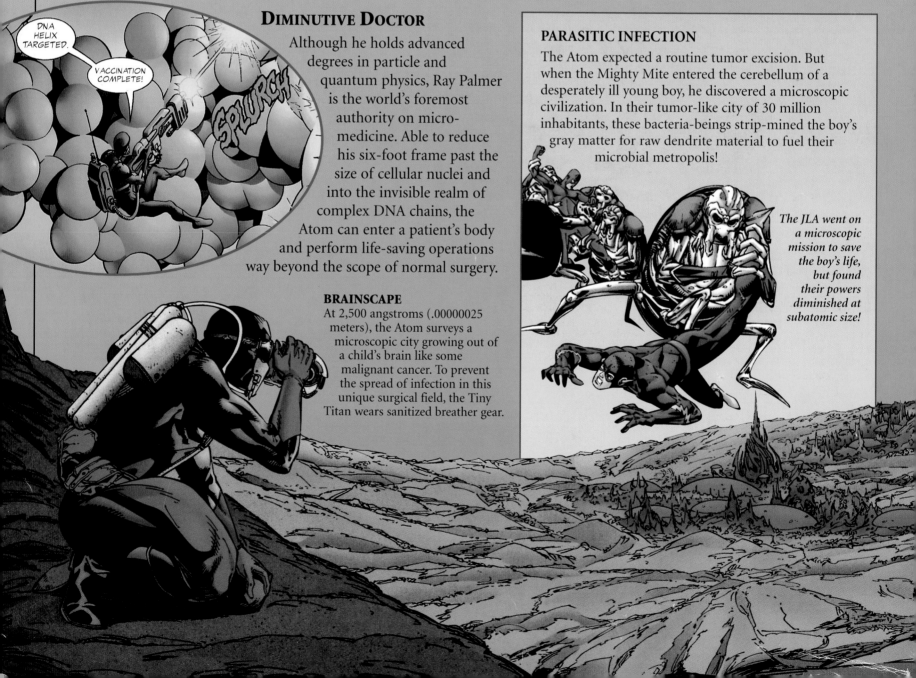

MINI HERO

The Atom wields complete control over his size, weight, and mass, from his standard six feet to infinitesimal proportions registering only on powerful electron microscopes. Prior to the advent of cellular phone technology, the Atom traveled via telephone land-lines, shrinking to subatomic size and "surfing" electronic impulses between receivers.

REAL NAME
Raymond "Ray" Palmer

OCCUPATION
Physics Professor

BASE Ivytown

HEIGHT 6 ft **WEIGHT** 180 lb

EYES Brown **HAIR** Auburn

FIRST APPEARANCE
SHOWCASE #34
(September-October 1961)

The Atom's costume is visible only during miniaturization.

Controls in glove alter the Atom's size and relative weight.

FALL ALREADY! FALL!

POOM

POOM

EAR DRUMMED
Don't underestimate the power of the Atom. Stealthy and undetectable, this speck-sized hero is suited to espionage and attacking an enemy from within… literally! While on a mission to save Superman's life from kryptonite poisoning, the Atom entered the inner ear of the contract killer Deathstroke, pummeling the assassin's tympanic membrane to agonizing advantage.

AIIIGH!

Even reduced to 6-in size, the Atom can pack a 180-lb wallop!

TINY TRUTHS
When the vengeful Rama Khan used sorcery to unravel the fabric of truth binding reality together, the Atom helped the Justice League understand the potential catastrophe facing Earth. Ray Palmer was working in his Ivy University microscopic lab when Khan's arcane assault took place, reducing the rational physicist to near-madness as the most rudimentary mathematics stopped making sense!

The Atom lectures his JLA teammates on how the breakdown of scientific truth brings chaos.

ZAURIEL

JLA

A GUARDIAN ANGEL of Heaven's Eagle-Host, the winged Zauriel forsook his exalted perch in the Silver City after falling in love with his mortal charge. Zauriel left Heaven pursued by forces loyal to Asmodel, the renegade King-Angel of the Bull-Host. Zauriel alone knew of Asmodel's planned coup to divide and conquer Heaven itself! Falling to Earth, Zauriel found kindred spirits in the Justice League. In a near-apocalyptic battle, Asmodel was routed and sent straight to the fiery depths of Hell for his sins. Zauriel, meanwhile, kept his wings and his place in the Justice League.

Beneath the warm Pacific waters off the coast of San Francisco – briefly his home on Earth – Zauriel met J'onn J'onzz.

ASMODEL

Of Heaven's four Angel Hosts in the Pax Dei, the Cherubim Alpha Battalion of Asmodel far surpassed the Eagle, Lion, and Human Seraphim in hubris and militancy. Asmodel himself was ten feet tall, with a gaze that could sear flesh from bone and whose blood was the universal solvent. One beat of his heart was as thunderous as a thousand atomic bombs!

LEAGUE ARCHIVIST

During his brief membership of the JLA, Zauriel eagerly volunteered to be team historian, documenting the League's many epic adventures. He also took on the role of Trophy Room curator, cataloging the mementos on display.

HHNNNN!

KKKKKHHHHHII!

ANGELIC ATTRIBUTES

Although forced to renounce his immortality, Zauriel left the Silver City with his holy strength and heavenly armor – inscribed with protective glyphs – intact. He also wields a formidable flaming sword. But his most unique gift is a scream that can shatter steel or disintegrate the bodies of betraying Bull-Angels, robbing them of material form in the Earthly plane.

Zauriel can fly at incredible speeds.

THE WRATH OF GOD

When the fifth-dimensional sprite QWSP influenced the hero Triumph into betraying his former JLA teammates, Zauriel came to the forgotten JLA founder's defense against the Spectre. As God's Spirit of Wrath on Earth, the Spectre – also a member of the JSA – transformed the turncoat Triumph into a pillar of ice, which he intended to smash to smithereens!

HEAVEN AND EARTH UNITE!

As the end of everything approached during Mageddon's attack, Zauriel did what an angel should… he died so others might live. With the Watchtower booby-trapped by the Injustice Gang, Zauriel gave his teammates time to evacuate, but was consumed in a thermonuclear fire. His spirit pleaded humanity's cause in Heaven. As Mageddon neared Earth, Zauriel convinced the angels of the Pax Dei to fight for Heaven *and* Earth.

REAL NAME Zauriel
OCCUPATION Guardian Angel
BASE The Silver City
HEIGHT 6 ft 1 in
WEIGHT 180 lb
EYES Purple and Red
HAIR Silver
FIRST APPEARANCE
JLA #6 (June 1997)

The Huntress's arsenal includes crossbow bolts, throwing knives, and CO_2-propelled darts fired from a "wrist-bow" gauntlet on her right forearm.

LEAGUE ASSOCIATES
JLA

THERE IS NO GREATER HONOR than to belong to the Justice League of America. This distinction is regarded with pride and also with humility by those few costumed champions who have been invited to sit at the League's hallowed round table. The nuclear-powered Firestorm was the JLA's youngest member, while the Huntress was perhaps its most volatile. Hourman – a synthetic man from the 853rd century – was the Justice League's third android associate (after Red Tornado and Tomorrow Woman). And Aztek was undoubtedly one of the team's most noble heroes, giving his life in the epic battle to save Earth from Mageddon.

FIRESTORM

Two were united as one when an explosion at the Hudson Nuclear Facility fused physicist Martin Stein and high-school student Ronnie Raymond into a single flame-haired being. Able to merge at will – Ronnie controlling the body and Professor Stein advising in spirit form – the pair became Firestorm, a flying, matter-transmuting junior member of the JLA. Stein and Raymond later separated, however Ronnie retains the powers of Firestorm and still aids the League on occasion.

HUNTRESS

As a child, Helena Bertinelli witnessed the murders of her mob-connected crime family. Helena dedicated her life to one day destroying the Gotham City Mafioso as the relentless Huntress. Helena's violent methods placed her at odds with Gotham's resident vigilante, Batman. But it was the Dark Knight who nominated the Huntress for JLA membership, hoping that time with the League would help her learn restraint. However, the uncompromising Huntress was ousted after threatening to kill Prometheus.

BOLT FROM THE BLUE
Huntress's well-aimed crossbow bolt saves the feline fatale Catwoman from one of Prometheus's deadly darts!

HOURMAN

Forged in the 853rd century, Hourman is an advanced android imprinted with the genetic signature of 20th-century chemist Rex Tyler. During World War II, Tyler became the heroic "Hourman," his strength, speed, and stamina enhanced for 60 minutes by his Miraclo Pill. Tyler's futuristic namesake inherited this ability, first meeting the JLA during their time-hopping trek to wrest the Worlogog from Luthor's Injustice Gang.

> DIE!
> ...LIKE EVERYONE ELSE WHO CROSSES MY PATH!
> FLASH--?

ECLIPSED!
Hourman became guardian of the reality-altering Worlogog. He later aided the JLA in thwarting the tyrant sun Solaris and then freed the Flash from forcibly reliving the JLA's greatest crises – including domination by the evil-inducing Eclipso (above).

Prior to JLA induction, Aztek proved his mettle by battling one of the League's oldest foes, an upgraded Amazo android!

Aztek's helmet harnessed 4-dimensional energy and contained the collective knowledge of all its previous wearers.

AZTEK

For a millennium, the shadowy Q Foundation prepared for the apocalyptic return of the Aztec shadow god Tezcatlipoca by empowering a champion to save the world. Uno was the most recent defender, donning the mantle of Aztek while disguised as Dr. Curt Falconer. Aztek's heroic exploits earned him JLA membership. However, after learning that Lex Luthor had funded his training, he resigned. Uno died trying to destroy Mageddon, hoping that his sacrifice redeemed his connection to Luthor.

New Gods

JLA

On the "Fourth World" of New Genesis and its dark twin Apokolips, they are known as New Gods. Longtime allies of the Justice League, Orion and Big Barda have often helped thwart the machinations of Apokolips' dread lord Darkseid. At the behest of Takion, Highfather of New Genesis, Orion and Barda became ambassadors to Earth, joining the JLA to fortify its ranks against the coming of Mageddon!

Blaster cannons unleash Orion's destructive Astro-Force.

THE BLOOD RED GAME OF GODS HAS BEGUN!

Astro-Glider enables shielded travel through space at incredible speeds.

SON OF DARKSEID
For millennia, New Genesis and Apokolips have been at war. Orion, the scion of the evil Darkseid, was traded with the son of the New Genesian Highfather Izaya to secure a tentative peace.

CHOOM!

ORION THE HUNTER
Although raised on peaceful New Genesis, Orion is Apokoliptian through and through. New Genesian Mother Box computers help calm Orion's savagery, but not his impetuousness. While with the League, super-strong Orion often charged into battle without considering the consequences.

NYAAAAARR!

STURMER
While living on the Watchtower, Orion brought along a faithful friend from New Genesis. Sturmer was pack commander of the New Genesian Dog Cavalry. The tenacious canine was last seen bounding upon the General, sending both tumbling into the Ghost Zone.

THE DOG OF WAR!
When a single White Martian slipped his telepathic bonds, the alien made short work of the League members sent to recapture him. But not the teammates from New Genesis. As Barda doused Orion with gasoline and set him aflame, the unfortunate White Martian learned why the fast-healing son of Darkseid is known far and wide as "The Dog of War."

BIG BARDA

Barda Free was raised on dismal Apokolips, one of many urchins consigned to the orphanages of cruel Granny Goodness. Barda was trained by Granny herself to lead the Female Furies, Darkseid's elite battalion of women warriors, but rebelled when she met and fell in love with the son of Highfather.

CHAINS OF LOVE
No longer a slave to Apokolips, Barda is happily married to Scott Free, a.k.a. Mister Miracle, the Fourth World's greatest escape artist and a former Justice League member himself.

SPARRING PARTNER
Of all the JLA members, Barda found most kinship with Wonder Woman, who, like her, was schooled from childhood in martial skills. The two sharpened their battle readiness by sparring in the League's gymnasium.

WHUNNTCH!

NNNEEUUU!

STINGING THE QUEEN
Where Orion is impulsive in combat, Big Barda is more calculating. Under the tutelage of Granny Goodness, Barda mastered all forms of warfare and weaponry. The Queen Bee once felt the power of Barda's preferred weapon, the Mega-Rod, an Apokliptic device capable increasing gravitational forces or shredding metal with its energy bolts. As well, Barda wears aero-discs on her feet to enable flight.

THE JSA

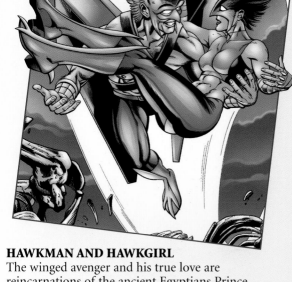

THE SO-CALLED "MYSTERY MEN" of the late 1930s arose just as World War II pitted the democratic Allied nations against the fascists and dictators of the dreaded Axis powers. Actively combating crime as individuals, America's colorfully costumed crimebusters first assembled in 1940 at the behest of President Roosevelt to form a super-powered "Justice Battalion" to beat back Adolf Hitler's planned invasion of England at Dover. After helping to rout the Nazis, the original Atom, Dr. Fate, Flash, Green Lantern, Hawkman, Hourman, Sandman, and the Spectre remained united as the world's first super-hero alliance, the Justice Society of America!

JUSTICE REINCORPORATED

Despite its service to America and mankind, the Justice Society was forced into retirement in 1951, a victim of the "communist witch-hunting" House of Representatives Un-American Activities Committee. The team would later join its JLA successors on a semi-regular basis to combat Earth-threatening crises, eventually forming a new pan-generational JSA.

MR. TERRIFIC

The first Mr. Terrific was the late Terry Sloane, a multitalented prodigy who espoused "fair play" as he fought crime. Sloane's successor is Michael Holt, an Olympic decathlon gold medallist who uses his athletic prowess and information-gathering T-spheres to bring fair play into New York's crime-ridden inner city.

HAWKMAN AND HAWKGIRL

The winged avenger and his true love are reincarnations of the ancient Egyptians Prince Khufu and his true love Chay-Ara. They were exposed to the anti-gravity Nth metal from Thanagar and imprinted with latent racial memories of that distant planet's people. Reborn time and again through the ages, Khufu and Chay-Ara are currently known as Carter Hall and Kendra Sanders, the high-flying Hawkman and Hawkgirl!

The JSA currently includes (left to right): Mr. Terrific, Sentinel, Dr. Mid-Nite, Sand, Hawkman, Hawkgirl, Atom-Smasher, Dr. Fate, Flash, Star-Spangled Kid, Black Canary, and Wildcat.

SENTINEL

Alan Scott may have ceded the official title of Green Lantern to Kyle Rayner, but this elder statesmen of super-heroics continues to shed his emerald light upon dark evil as Sentinel. Having absorbed the energies of the Starheart, Scott no longer needs a ring or battery of power to fight the good fight.

WILDCAT

Ex-heavyweight champ Ted Grant knuckle-dusted supervillains as Wildcat after being forced out of the boxing ring in the 1940s. One of the JSA's oldest members, Wildcat has trained several latter-day vigilantes – including the JLA's Batman and Black Canary – in the "sweet science" of fisticuffs. Wildcat's continued vitality is a result of age-retarding temporal magicks sorcerer Ian Karkull once unleashed upon the JSA during an early adventure. However, the nature of Grant's death-defying "nine lives" has yet to be explained.

Wildcat and Black Canary, with Soseh Mykros (a.k.a. the scimitar-brandishing Nemesis) hunt the Ultra-Humanite, a longtime foe of the JSA!

WHAK

THE FLASH

Jay Garrick was just a college student in 1938 when he inadvertently inhaled the potent vapors of radioactive "hard water" and was forever connected to the velocity-charged Speed Force. As the Flash, Garrick still pursues the criminals of Keystone City, while remaining an inspiration and advisor to several subsequent super-speedsters.

The Speed Force infuses the seventy-something Jay Garrick with turbo-charged vim and vigor!

STAR ROCKET RACER

Although most of the JSA members were "old-timers" when space travel was still merely the stuff of science fiction, the veteran heroes now escape Earth's gravity aboard the stylish Star Rocket Racer, built and maintained by Pat Dugan, once the costumed adult sidekick Stripesy to the first Star-Spangled Kid. The SSR saw action most recently during the galaxy-spanning Imperiex War.

Young Guns

JLA

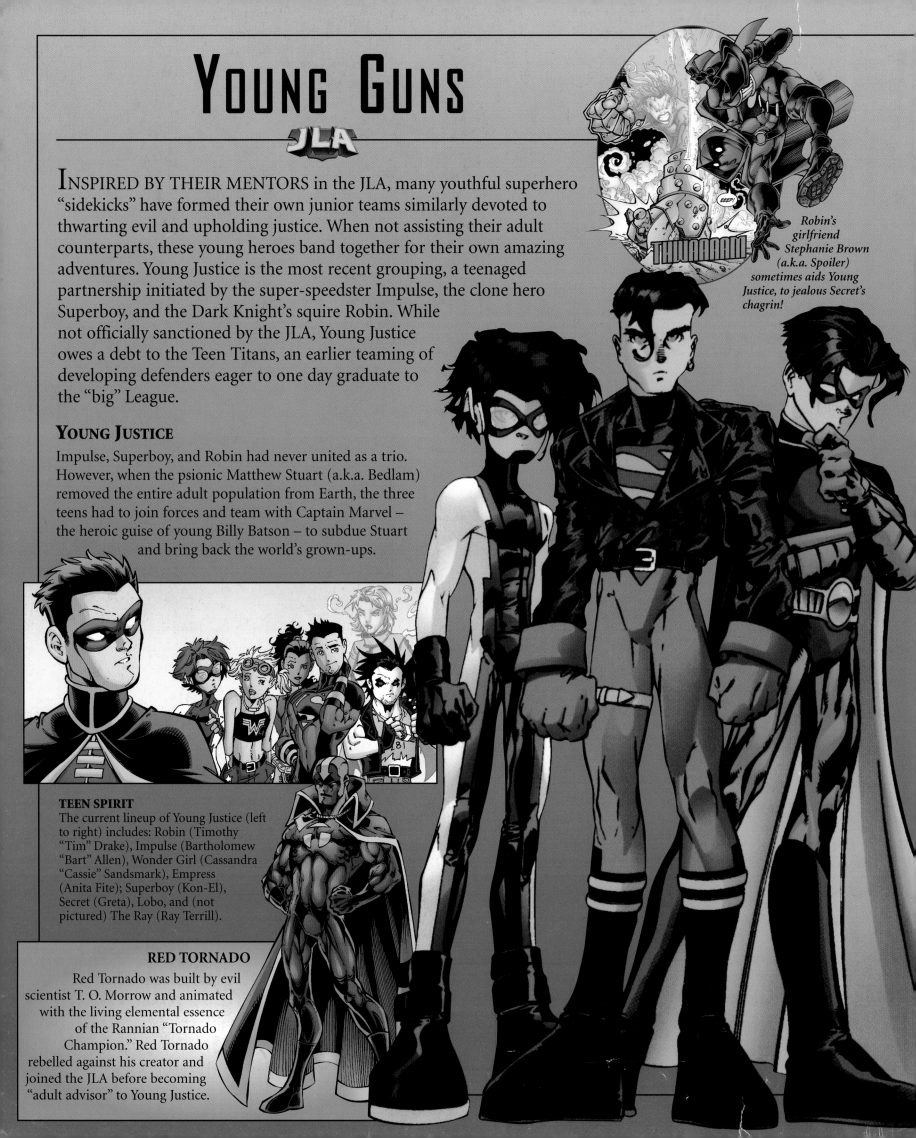

INSPIRED BY THEIR MENTORS in the JLA, many youthful superhero "sidekicks" have formed their own junior teams similarly devoted to thwarting evil and upholding justice. When not assisting their adult counterparts, these young heroes band together for their own amazing adventures. Young Justice is the most recent grouping, a teenaged partnership initiated by the super-speedster Impulse, the clone hero Superboy, and the Dark Knight's squire Robin. While not officially sanctioned by the JLA, Young Justice owes a debt to the Teen Titans, an earlier teaming of developing defenders eager to one day graduate to the "big" League.

Robin's girlfriend Stephanie Brown (a.k.a. Spoiler) sometimes aids Young Justice, to jealous Secret's chagrin!

YOUNG JUSTICE

Impulse, Superboy, and Robin had never united as a trio. However, when the psionic Matthew Stuart (a.k.a. Bedlam) removed the entire adult population from Earth, the three teens had to join forces and team with Captain Marvel – the heroic guise of young Billy Batson – to subdue Stuart and bring back the world's grown-ups.

TEEN SPIRIT

The current lineup of Young Justice (left to right) includes: Robin (Timothy "Tim" Drake), Impulse (Bartholomew "Bart" Allen), Wonder Girl (Cassandra "Cassie" Sandsmark), Empress (Anita Fite); Superboy (Kon-El), Secret (Greta), Lobo, and (not pictured) The Ray (Ray Terrill).

RED TORNADO

Red Tornado was built by evil scientist T. O. Morrow and animated with the living elemental essence of the Rannian "Tornado Champion." Red Tornado rebelled against his creator and joined the JLA before becoming "adult advisor" to Young Justice.

STARFIRE

Princess Koriand'r of Tamaran joined the Teen Titans after seeking asylum on Earth while eluding the reptilian Gordanian slavers of the despotic Citadel. As Starfire, Koriand'r absorbs solar energy to enable flight and emit searing starbolts. She has since departed the Titans to lead the refugees of her destroyed homeworld.

3X2(9YZ) 4A!

JESSE QUICK

Jesse Chambers is the daughter of Johnny Chambers (a.k.a. Johnny Quick) and Libby Lawrence (a.k.a. Liberty Belle). Like her father, Jesse gains super-speed and flight when she recites the speed formula "3X2(9YZ)4A." Like her mother, Jesse is capable of bursts of super-strength.

SEE, THE THING ABOUT ME IS, I CAN USE ANYTHING AS A WEAPON.

SO THE MORE YOU BLAST STUFF APART, THE MORE WEAPONS YOU GIVE ME.

ARSENAL

As a boy, Roy Harper was known as "Speedy," associate archer to the Green Arrow. In manhood, Harper targets criminals as the hero Arsenal, using his mastery of the martial art of Moo-Gi-Gon to turn any object into a precision weapon.

THE TITANS

The first Robin (Dick Grayson), Aqualad (Garth), Kid Flash (Wally West) Wonder Girl (Donna Troy), and Speedy saved the world when they freed the JLA from the Antithesis. Today, the Titans have new identities. Robin is Nightwing, Aqualad brandishes water-based powers as Tempest, while Wonder Girl remains an Amazonian powerhouse as Troia. The Titans also lists Arsenal, Jesse Quick, and the plasma-powered Argent in its lineup.

Enemies of the League

JLA

Evil wears many faces… and the Justice League has seen most of them, beating back scores of extraterrestrials determined to dominate Earth or destroy it. From the will-sapping Star Conqueror and the marauding White Martians to the hate-mongering Mageddon and insectoid Queen Bee, the Justice League's alien foes have fully tested the members' power and purpose. While threats from without continue to concern the League, there remain enemies from within – Earth-born scourges convinced of their right to rule the planet! Lex Luthor commands the Injustice Gang, a confederation of the JLA's nemeses. The Key has unlocked the potential of his own mind to enslave mankind. Prometheus worships at the altar of anarchy, celebrating evil as he targets heroes for murder. The Queen of Fables has turned her own vanity into a centuries-spanning vendetta. And there are still more: secret societies of villainy, techno-tyrants, and immortal terrors – even the devil himself! Any one of them would gladly bring chaos and doom to Earth. Thankfully, the JLA won't let them.

THE STAR CONQUEROR

JLA

THEY CALLED IT "STARRO" in an ironic nod to its probes' superficial resemblance to harmless Earthly starfish. Unfortunately, the Star Conqueror was anything but benign. In fact, this eons-old extraterrestrial menace was really a collective consciousness that drifted through the cosmos dividing and conquering. Starro replicated itself a trillion times over with face-sucking probes enslaving the populations of entire worlds. Earth would have been next if not for the Justice League. Though disbanded, the super heroes gathered together once more to save their planet from a fate far worse than death could ever be.

FLASH ENCOUNTERS STARRO

Strangely, the Star Conqueror's beachhead for occupying Earth was Blue Valley, Nebraska, a Midwestern hamlet far from any nurturing ocean. It also happened to be Wally West's hometown! Thus, the Flash was the first hero to respond to the alien invasion. The Scarlet Speedster raced headlong into a school of Starro probes!

Even the fleet-footed Flash was halted in his tracks when faced with the enormity of the Star Conqueror!

LANTERN RAMPAGE

The JLA had to do something. But the Spectre – God's Earthbound Spirit of Wrath – forbade the heroes to intervene. The Spectre revealed a future where the Justice League marched across the cosmos as the Star Conqueror's super-powered soldiery!

REAL NAME	Inapplicable
OCCUPATION	Alien Invader
HOMEWORLD	Unknown
HEIGHT	Variable
WEIGHT	Variable
EYES	Red sclera with yellow pupil
SKIN	Olive Green
FIRST APPEARANCE	JLA SECRET FILES #1 (September 1997)

FUTURE TENSE

Within the Spectre's cloak, the JLA not only witnessed the Star Conqueror's domination of the universe, they *lived* it! The heroes realized that the only way to defeat Starro would be to relinquish their extraordinary abilities. Magically, the Spectre stripped the League members of their powers. The Star Conqueror expected metahuman resistance, laying a trap for super-powered defenders. But the JLA simply responded with good old-fashioned teamwork, freeing the Flash and the rest of Blue Valley from Starro's thrall!

CONTINENTAL DRIFT

Starro didn't give up on Earth so easily. The Star Conqueror's second wave circumvented the waking world, this time attacking Earth's denizens in their sleep. Even the JLA was oblivious until the Sandman, King of Dreams, roused the team to the renewed threat. Within the Dreaming realm, the JLA met young Michael Haney, a solitary holdout against Starro's subjugation of an unconscious planet.

WORLD DOMINATION

Trapped within the Dreaming, Michael Haney never stopped believing that the Justice League would rescue him from Starro. As Superman, Green Lantern, and Wonder Woman battled the Conqueror's probes in dreamtime, J'onn J'onzz witnessed the Star Conqueror's true horror in the waking world!

I CAN SEE IT.

WE'RE ALL ADULTS HERE, MR. WEST.

ALIEN AUTOPSY

With their powers diminished in the Dreaming, the JLA relied on its conscious teammates to defeat the Star Conqueror. By dissecting one of Starro's probes, Batman learned that the face-sucker was an organic signaling device. The JLA broadcast on the probe's frequency and convinced the Star Conqueror that Earth's environment was too hostile for its survival!

BOTTLED DREAMS

Michael Haney awoke when Starro withdrew its grip on the unconscious world. But Michael was no longer a little boy: he was a homeless military veteran, a forgotten hero who had helped save the world. The Sandman thanked Haney with a hatful of gold, then returned to the Dreaming with the Star Conqueror imprisoned inside a fishbowl. Starro now dreams of conquests it can never know.

WHITE MARTIANS
JLA

EONS AGO THEY DOMINATED neighboring Earth, cruel Martian invaders whose callous disregard for life brought environmental catastrophe. One of two disparate races populating the Red Planet, the Pale or "White Martians," were belligerent, bloodthirsty, and bipolar opposites of their peaceful Green Martian kin. In their rape of Earth, the White Martians set back superhuman evolution. And as punishment, they were imprisoned by the Green Martians within the interdimensional Still Zone. There they watched and waited, biding an eternity in anticipation of reclaiming Earth as their own!

HUMAN ANATOMY 101
Escaping from captivity, the White Martians once more engaged in vile vivisection. They stole brain matter from latent human telepaths in order to mutate and multiply their own terrible telepathic powers!

ALIEN ABILITIES

The White Martians wield a panoply of superpowers. In addition to laser-like "Martian Vision," flight, enhanced strength, super-speed, and telepathy, they are natural shape-shifters, able to change their appearance and density for camouflage or mimicry. The latter ability was crucial to their return from exile, enabling the White Martians to fool the peoples of Earth into believing them friends instead of foes.

REAL NAMES Unpronounceable
OCCUPATION Alien Occupiers
BASE The Still Zone
HEIGHT Variable
WEIGHT Variable
EYES Red **SKIN** Chalk White
FIRST APPEARANCE
(As Hyperclan) JLA #1
(January 1997)

Morphing his fearsome features, a White Martian takes on the identity of billionaire Bruce Wayne!

Tronix

A-Mortal

Armek

Fluxus

> I AM PROTEX. WE ARE THE HYPERCLAN.
>
> WE'VE COME TO SAVE THE WORLD.

Zenturion

Züm

Primaid

THE HYPERCLAN

Extricating themselves from the Still Zone (also known as the Ghost Zone or Phantom Zone), the White Martians returned to Earth in the guise of gods calling themselves the Hyperclan. The Martians claimed their homeworld had been destroyed by negligence and greed and they offered to save Earth from a similar fate, succeeding where the JLA could not. The Hyperclan turned deserts into verdant paradises and ended crime by executing meta-criminals… all part of their insidious plan to discredit and destroy the Justice League!

The Hyperclan used their Martian abilities to create the illusion of being super-powered saviors from another world!

MARTIAN REUNION

The JLA defeated the Hyperclan with fire, a Martian weakness. J'onn J'onzz then "mind-wiped" the White Martians, leaving them in human form with no knowledge of their past. However, J'onn's encounter with the wish-granting Id made the sole surviving Green Martian yearn for company and unconsciously awaken his cruel cousins!

> WHERE IS J'ONN? WHAT HAVE YOU DONE WITH HIM?
>
> WHERE IS HE?

> SAY "AAAAAAAH!"

FIGHTING WITH FIRE

Determined to forestall any resistance, the White Martians seeded Earth's atmosphere with subatomic particles that inhibited any combustible reaction. No longer fearful of fire, the White Martians imprisoned the JLA in the Still Zone. But the League escaped, nullified the particles and lured the aliens to the Watchtower. The White Martians met defeat as the Moon itself was set aflame!

MAGEDDON

EVERY CIVILIZATION has a name for it. The Anti-Sun. The Primordial Annihilator. The Old Dragon. The Ultimate Warbringer. On peaceful New Genesis, home of the New Gods, it was called "Mageddon," a name uttered only in hushed whispers because it foretold galactic destruction. In a forgotten time – well before the birth of the universe – Mageddon was created by the Old Gods of Urgrund, beings who destroyed themselves with weapons capable of rending infinity to pieces. Mageddon survived. After 15 billion years chained in a gravity sink on the outer curve of spacetime, it crawled from its prison and lurched across the cosmos toward Earth!

"NOW THERE *IS* NO DOUBT."

"BEHOLD MAGEDDON."

THE ULTIMATE WARBRINGER
Knowman warned the JLA about Mageddon, the Ultimate Warbringer, but only after the League stymied his attempts to transform mankind into super-powered metahumans. With Knowman's unnatural evolution halted, the Justice League was Earth's last hope against annihilation!

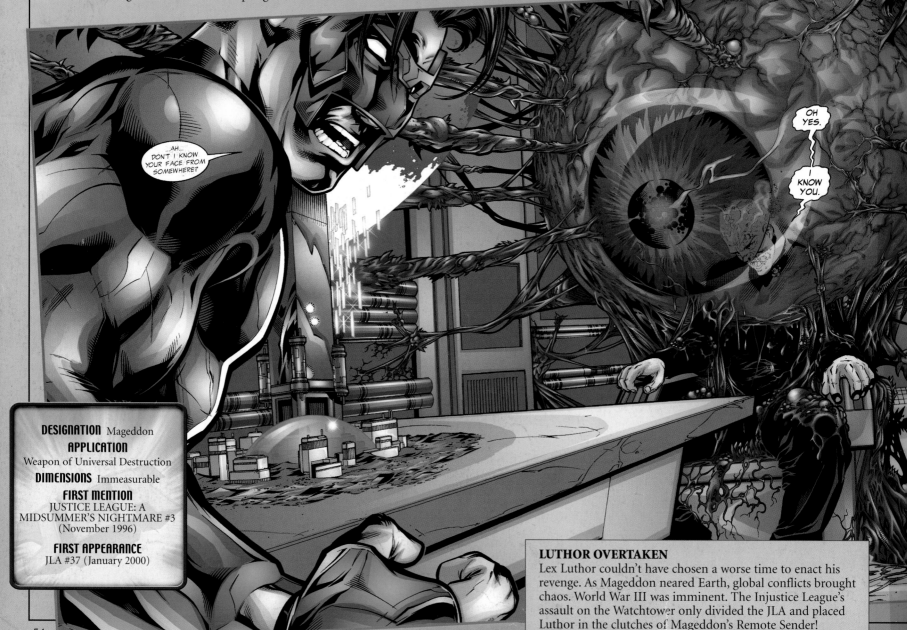

...AH... DON'T I KNOW YOUR FACE FROM SOMEWHERE?

OH YES.

I KNOW YOU.

DESIGNATION Mageddon
APPLICATION
Weapon of Universal Destruction
DIMENSIONS Immeasurable
FIRST MENTION
JUSTICE LEAGUE: A MIDSUMMER'S NIGHTMARE #3
(November 1996)
FIRST APPEARANCE
JLA #37 (January 2000)

LUTHOR OVERTAKEN
Lex Luthor couldn't have chosen a worse time to enact his revenge. As Mageddon neared Earth, global conflicts brought chaos. World War III was imminent. The Injustice League's assault on the Watchtower only divided the JLA and placed Luthor in the clutches of Mageddon's Remote Sender!

LUTHOR ESCAPES!

Luthor and the League realized that Mageddon's true power lay in unleashing mankind's repressed hostility and territorial aggression. Lex found himself serving as the Anti-Sun's unwilling "eye" on the cataclysm enveloping Earth. With a great effort, the Injustice Gang's leader shattered Mageddon's grip, nearly destroying his own mind in the process.

AZTEK'S SACRIFICE

The JLA suffered its first casualty in the core of the Mageddon warhead – primed to vaporize half the galaxy in apocalyptic fury. With Superman chained and powerless against the Anti-Sun, Aztek unleashed the full measure of energy in his armor. Though Mageddon's war machinery was unscathed, the young hero bought the Man of Steel precious time to free himself.

MIND MELD

Ex-JLA member Animal Man informed the League that Mageddon had triggered mankind's primitive R-complex. J'onn J'onzz vainly tried to reason telepathically with the Primordial Annihilator.

DOOMSDAY IS CANCELLED UNTIL FURTHER NOTICE. THE MAGEDDON WARHEAD HAS BEEN DISARMED.

ECLIPSE OF THE ANTI-SUN!

In the end, salvation lay in the armies of man, six billion strong and granted temporary superpowers by the JLA. As these "Justice League Reserves" attacked the Ultimate Warbringer, Superman dived into the heart of Mageddon. His solar-fueled body absorbed the anti-sunlight of the Mageddon warhead, preventing its doom-bringing detonation!

Queen Bee

Many light-years distant from Earth, the hiveworld Korll is home to Zazzala, Queen Bee to an insectoid race trillions strong – and *growing*. Countless worlds have fallen to the sting of Korllian expansion as the Queen Bee, Royal Genetrix of her swarming species, proliferates drone-slaves from galaxy to galaxy. Earth would eventually have been scented by Zazzala's advancing Bee-Troopers, but Lex Luthor hastened her majesty's subjugation of the planet by inviting the Queen Bee to join his Injustice Gang. Although her previous conquests had offered little resistance, she found the Justice League to be less eager to join her colony!

Multifaceted eyes register ultraviolet light.

Gauntlet contains barbed stingers in reflexive venom sacs.

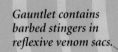

Muscles in abdominal trachea pump air through spiracles and trabeculae to keep Zazzala cool when inside the egg-matrix.

The Swarm Approaches

While the Injustice Gang plotted mankind's ruin, Zazzala's apian armada journeyed through "The Honeycomb," the region of infinitely compressed space known to Prometheus as "The Ghost Zone." Massing Bee-Troopers buzzed above Earth in eager anticipation of the techno-pheromone signaling their order to attack!

REAL NAME	Zazzala
OCCUPATION	Royal Genetrix
BASE	Korll
HEIGHT	5 ft 9 in
WEIGHT	226 lb
EYES Blue	**HAIR** Gray/Black
FIRST APPEARANCE	
JLA #34 (October 1999)	

DRONE TROOPERS
In the Korllian hierarchy, Bee-Troopers rank highest after Zazzala herself. These exclusively male warrior drones, raised in crèches of two hundred or more, are utterly loyal to the Royal Genetrix. Heavily armored and wielding bioelectric stinger cannons, the Bee-Troopers will gladly sacrifice their brief lives in service to the alluring Queen Bee.

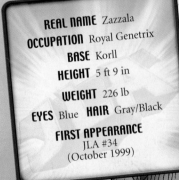

NEW HIVE CITY
Zazzala's subjugation of Earth began with New York City. The Big Apple's diverse populace quickly became the Queen Bee's drone-slaves when exposed to her mind-numbing hypno-pollen. As Zazzala commenced her plunder, street refuse and virtually any object not nailed down was scooped up by the drones to construct a megalithic Royal Egg-Matrix in the heart of downtown Manhattan!

THE COLOR OF DEFEAT
Only Plastic Man knew the key to the Queen Bee's defeat. While befriending a hero known as the Red Bee, Plas learned that his comrade's insect namesakes were blind to the color red. The JLA's response team – Plas, Wonder Woman, and the crimson-cloaked Barda and Steel – was well suited to ridding the Big Apple of its newest insect pest!

APIAN ALLIANCE
To gain the firepower of Queen Bee's marauding swarm, Luthor promised Zazzala a percentage of Earth's population to serve as her drone-slaves. Pausing just long enough to pluck the General from asteroid exile on 433 Eros, Zazzala brought with her the full force of Korll's colonial army to surround the Earth. While the world's heroes were occupied beating back this alien attack, Luthor's newest gangsters – The General, Prometheus, and Zazzala herself – sneaked through Prometheus's Ghost Zone to attack the JLA from within its own Watchtower!

INSECT REPELLANT
While Barda took the brunt of the Queen Bee's sting, Wonder Woman and Plastic Man kept her Bee-Trooper's busy long enough for Steel to activate a Boom Tube and teleport Zazzala and her swarm back to the hiveworld!

THE GENERAL

JLA

AIR FORCE GENERAL Wade Eiling never trusted super heroes or any other costumed metahumans. Decades ago, he initiated the Captain Atom Project, which transformed Captain Nathaniel Adam into a super-powered operative for the U.S. government. When the altruistic Captain Atom resigned, Eiling created the murderous Major Force. Eiling's obsession with maintaining a metahuman "balance of power" led to the recruitment of the Ultramarines Corps. However, unbeknownst to all, the General had a maniacal desire to gain superpowers for himself!

THE SHAGGY MAN AND THE GENERAL
When Eiling learned he had an inoperable brain tumor, he enlisted the Ultramarines to find a replacement body. Eiling's choice was the Shaggy Man! Created by Professor Andrew Zagarian out of adaptive "plastalloy," the Shaggy Man possessed vast strength and miraculous tissue regenerative abilities. It was more than a match for the JLA and the perfect vessel for the General to ensure his own longevity!

REAL NAME	Wade Eiling
OCCUPATION	Militant Monster
BASE	Mobile
HEIGHT	10 ft 5 in
WEIGHT	1,378 lb
EYES Red	**HAIR** Brown

FIRST APPEARANCE
(As Shaggy Man) JLA #25
(January 1999)

BODY SNATCHED
To defeat the first Shaggy Man, the JLA helped Professor Zagarian create a *second* Shaggy monster! One of the behemoths was later imprisoned by Aquaman in a Pacific Ocean trench. There, the Ultramarines found their quarry as General Eiling prepared for a new lease on life.

SPLURCH

SKZZAH!

UNBREAKABLE
Thanks to Professor Zagarian's "plastalloy" compound, the Shaggy Man could re-grow severed limbs and recover from any injury in minutes. Eiling used the same synthetic metagene that empowered the Ultramarines to transfer his own consciousness into Zagarian's monstrous invention.

PURRRR

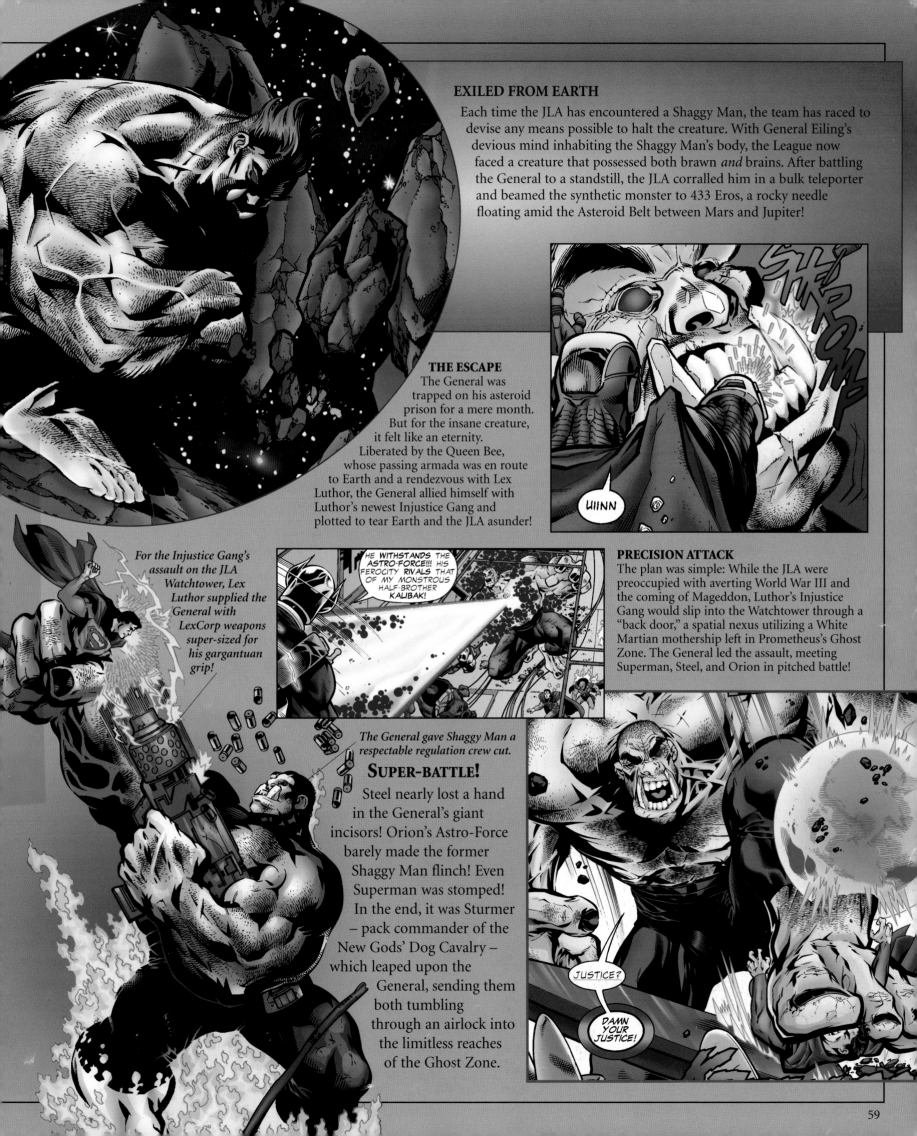

EXILED FROM EARTH

Each time the JLA has encountered a Shaggy Man, the team has raced to devise any means possible to halt the creature. With General Eiling's devious mind inhabiting the Shaggy Man's body, the League now faced a creature that possessed both brawn *and* brains. After battling the General to a standstill, the JLA corralled him in a bulk teleporter and beamed the synthetic monster to 433 Eros, a rocky needle floating amid the Asteroid Belt between Mars and Jupiter!

THE ESCAPE

The General was trapped on his asteroid prison for a mere month. But for the insane creature, it felt like an eternity. Liberated by the Queen Bee, whose passing armada was en route to Earth and a rendezvous with Lex Luthor, the General allied himself with Luthor's newest Injustice Gang and plotted to tear Earth and the JLA asunder!

For the Injustice Gang's assault on the JLA Watchtower, Lex Luthor supplied the General with LexCorp weapons super-sized for his gargantuan grip!

HE WITHSTANDS THE ASTRO-FORCE!!! HIS FEROCITY RIVALS THAT OF MY MONSTROUS HALF-BROTHER KALIBAK!

PRECISION ATTACK

The plan was simple: While the JLA were preoccupied with averting World War III and the coming of Mageddon, Luthor's Injustice Gang would slip into the Watchtower through a "back door," a spatial nexus utilizing a White Martian mothership left in Prometheus's Ghost Zone. The General led the assault, meeting Superman, Steel, and Orion in pitched battle!

The General gave Shaggy Man a respectable regulation crew cut.

SUPER-BATTLE!

Steel nearly lost a hand in the General's giant incisors! Orion's Astro-Force barely made the former Shaggy Man flinch! Even Superman was stomped! In the end, it was Sturmer – pack commander of the New Gods' Dog Cavalry – which leaped upon the General, sending them both tumbling through an airlock into the limitless reaches of the Ghost Zone.

JUSTICE?

DAMN YOUR JUSTICE!

59

THE INJUSTICE GANG

THE CRIMINAL CONSORTIUM known as "The Injustice Gang" is a loose alliance of super-villainy funded by Lex Luthor for one purpose: to destroy the Justice League of America! The Gang's original roster – Luthor, Catwoman, Sinestro, Dr. Light, The Penguin, Chronos, Black Manta, Mr. Element, and Felix Faust – was united by the extra-terrestrial Agamemno. And though this Injustice Gang was thwarted in its bid for global domination, Luthor realized that a properly managed legion of doom had unlimited potential. To that end, the Metropolis mogul continues to back the Injustice Gang's evil enterprises.

DISSENSION IN THE RANKS

Luthor ensures his continuing leadership of the Injustice Gang through intimidation and sheer force of will. Of course, possessing a mind-controlling piezoelectrical crystal helped to keep Luthor's Gangsters in line, including humbling a Clown Prince of Crime more interested in creating general havoc than the Injustice Gang's hostile takeover of the world.

MALICIOUS MERGER

When the JLA reconvened with seven of its most powerful members, Lex Luthor responded by assembling an Injustice Gang of the heroes' most diabolical adversaries. Joining him were the maniacal Joker, Ocean Master, Dr. Light, Circe, Mirror Master, and a mysterious seventh member – the Saturnian hero J'emm – kept in thrall to Luthor by the Worlogog, an alien artifact of unlimited power. With this so-called Philosopher's Stone and a new alliance, Luthor set out to divide and conquer the League.

Lex Luthor

Ocean Master

Circe

Mirror Master

The Joker

Doctor Light

Secretly built by LexCorp's aerospace division, the Injustice Gang's skull-shaped satellite headquarters stealthily orbited Earth.

LEADER Lex Luthor
MEMBERSHIP
Doctor Light, The Joker,
Mirror Master, Circe, Ocean Master
FIRST APPEARANCE
JLA #10 (September 1997)
INJUSTICE GANG 2.0
The General, Prometheus,
The Queen Bee
FIRST APPEARANCE
JLA #34 (October 1999)

...AND SEE THE WORLD AS THE JOKER SEES IT...

HA.

HA HA HA.

PARTNERS IN CRIME

Luthor conceals any formal connections to the Injustice Gang. For the billionaire businessman, the Gang is simply a means to the Justice League's end; he knows that partnerships with rogues like the psychotic Prometheus are precarious ventures at best, with little likelihood of capital gains.

TIME FOR THE NEW INJUSTICE GANG TO STRIKE THEN, WOULDN'T YOU SAY, LUTHOR?

YES, PROMETHEUS. I'D SAY IT'S TIME.

MIND GAMES

Luthor had successfully thinned the ranks of the JLA. As Aquaman, Flash, and Green Lantern fought to escape an Apokoliptic possible future, the League's newest member, Aztek, raced to disarm a dozen nuclear warheads teleported into the heart of the JLA Watchtower. Meanwhile, the JLA's most powerful members – Superman and J'onn J'onzz – found themselves trapped within a decoy of the Injustice Gang satellite and navigating a hard-light maze patterned on the Joker's labyrinthine lunacy!

FEMININE CHARMS

In Greek myth, the beautiful Circe transformed sailors who landed on her island into beasts. Lex Luthor recruited the sorceress to use her bewitching powers to make the young Green Arrow betray the JLA!

THE MOMENT IS OURS.

AND SO TO WAR.

INJUSTICE 2.0

After the defeat of his seven-strong Gang, Luthor recruited a smaller, but even more powerful team, comprising The General, Prometheus, and the Queen Bee. However, this Gang was also quickly defeated by the JLA. And now that Luthor is President of the United States, the Injustice Gang has been disbanded… for now.

THE KEY

Spinal harness delivers psycho-chemical injections into the Key's cerebral cortex.

Musculature atrophied during years comatose.

Key-shaped neural shock rifle.

Electronic "skeleton keys."

UNLOCKING THE BRAIN'S untapped potential has always been his primary motivation. As a chemist in the employ of Intergang, the man who would become "The Key" injected himself with experimental psycho-chemicals concocted to boost his own intellectual potential. Although rendering his senses hyper-aware, the Key's pharmacological evolution also revealed his monomaniacal obsession with ruling reality. Fortunately, the JLA has always barred the Key from securing this lofty ambition. Undaunted, the Key continues to seek the power necessary to unlock the door that would lead him to the total domination of Tomorrow!

ALTERED STATES

Despite elevating his mental capacity, the Key's psycho-chemicals ravaged his body over time. To expand his consciousness further – and avoid defeat by the Justice League – the Key forced himself into a catatonic state. His self-induced slumber was interrupted by the demon Neron, who traded the Key an even higher state of mind in exchange for what little remained of the criminal's soul.

With 11 hyper-actuated senses and an arsenal of universal "skeleton keys," the Key can pick any lock or unclasp any bond.

REAL NAME Unrevealed
OCCUPATION
Would-Be World Conqueror
BASE Mobile
HEIGHT 6 ft 1 in
WEIGHT 197 lb
EYES Red **HAIR** White
FIRST APPEARANCE
JUSTICE LEAGUE OF AMERICA
#41 (December 1965)

NEURAL SHOCK RIFLE

In addition to administering psychotropic drugs to control the minds of his victims, the Key also wields a formidable Neural Shock Rifle. Powerful enough to stagger the Man of Steel, the Key's NSR is an energy-based weapon designed to paralyze the central nervous system. At its highest setting, the Neural Shock Rifle can kill.

Insulated composite alloy barrel.

Promethium-coil focusing array.

Impact-resistant ceramic stock.

Bio-dendrite power source.

Beam range and dispersal controls.

Trigger coded to the Key's unique DNA signature.

After defeating the Watchtower's defenses, the Key blasts the JLA!

ATTACK OF THE KEY-MEN

The Key once trapped the JLA within artificial "dream lives" created by a programmable psycho-virus. The heroes escaped and prevented the Key from entering "The Lock," a doorway into negative space that would grant him unbridled power. The Key then loosed his clockwork Key-Men on the JLA!

THE ULTIMATE ESCAPE

To challenge Batman, the Key locked every door in Gotham City's Arkham Asylum and psycho-chemically unleashed the repressed rage inside the Dark Knight. As Robin succumbed to the same neural anti-inhibitors, the Key confessed his masterplan to the Boy Wonder: he wished to force Batman to murder him, so that he could escape life itself.

AND HERE'S THE TRULY *IMPRESSIVE* PART-- I THOUGHT TO MYSELF, "NO *DOORS*...THAT *IS* THE KEY! THAT'S THE *WHOLE* OF IT!" AND I MEAN THAT IN THE MOST PROFOUND SENSE *IMAGINABLE.*

PEOPLE *TALK* ABOUT THE "ONENESS OF THE UNIVERSE" BUT CAN YOU REALLY FATHOM WHAT THAT *MEANS* ON AN EMPYREAL OR EVEN VACUOLAR LEVEL?

PROMETHEUS
JLA

REAL NAME Unknown
OCCUPATION Hero-Hunter
BASE The Ghost Zone
HEIGHT 6 ft 1 in
WEIGHT 180 lb
EYES Brown **HAIR** White
FIRST APPEARANCE
PROMETHEUS #1
(December 1997)

Computerized helmet linked to central nervous system.

Helmet lights strobe to hypnotize or disorient opponents.

Armor is interlaced with synaptic relays that augment his formidable fighting prowess.

Energized nightstick can shatter steel and is designed to override shielded electronic systems.

CONSIDER THE DARKER KNIGHT in tarnished armor to be the "Anti-Batman." Bruce Wayne's parents were murdered by a vicious mugger. But the boy who became Prometheus was the orphaned son of a criminal couple gunned down in a hail of policemen's bullets! And where Wayne dedicated his life to warring on crime, Prometheus decided his path lay in targeting the forces of justice for annihilation. He very nearly succeeded. Stealthily stealing aboard the JLA's lunar Watchtower, Prometheus almost single-handedly destroyed the Justice League. Later, he joined forces with Lex Luthor's most recent Injustice Gang. On both occasions, Prometheus eluded capture. He might not be so lucky a *third* time.

CHILDHOOD TRAUMA
As long as Prometheus could remember, his parents were on the run and the cops were never far behind. Finally surrounded, his felonious family tried to shoot their way out. The shock of witnessing their deaths turned Prometheus's hair white and fueled his hatred of law enforcement.

ORIGINAL SIN

Left wealthy from his parents' criminal caches, Prometheus blackmailed a mob boss into creating a new identity for him. At 16, the vengeful youth traveled the world, undertaking rigorous academic study, while learning to maim and kill in every culture he encountered. His quest for knowledge and power led him to Tibet.

THE LAMA
Seeking the entrance to mythical Shamballa, a kingdom buried beneath Mongolia, Prometheus discovered an ancient sentient spaceship. After living for a time among Tibetan monks, he was led to the heart of Shamballa by an aged Lama, who granted him the Cosmic Key to a new home.

Childlike design belies sinister intent: the Crooked House contains an arsenal of high-tech weaponry.

To defeat Batman, Prometheus downloaded the fighting skills of 30 martial artists, including the Dark Knight himself, into his brain!

CROOKED HOUSE
Prometheus called it the Ghost Zone. Martians have long referred to it as the Still Zone. On Krypton this endless, inter-dimensional void was known infamously as the Phantom Zone. With his Cosmic Key allowing him unfettered access to a realm of nothingness that defied physical laws, Prometheus built a Crooked House befitting his own warped soul.

TINY BAUBLES
Prometheus prides himself on his ability to detect and exploit his enemies' weaknesses. As a member of the Injustice Gang, Prometheus engineered an uprising among the supervillain inmates of Louisiana's Belle Reve Penitentiary. As scores of metahuman criminals rioted, a loser known as the "Red Dart" managed to spirit away Green Lantern's power ring and place the glowing bauble in Prometheus's waiting hand.

PENETRATING THE WATCHTOWER
In Greek myth, the Titan Prometheus stole fire from the gods to give to mankind. The latter-day Prometheus possessed none of his namesake's altruism, attacking the JLA in their lunar Watchtower. He murdered the hero Retro, donned his costume, and entered via the League's teleportation tubes during a press visit to the team's headquarters. As the world's media looked on, Prometheus defeated the JLA one by one!

ACHILLES HEELS
He short-circuited Steel's armor. He beat Batman to a pulp. And after nearly immolating J'onn J'onzz with a phosphorous dart, he shot the Martian Manhunter with a toxin that paralyzed his nervous system.

WHO WANTS TO BE NUMBER SIX?

CHUFF!

THE QUEEN OF FABLES

JLA

BEDTIME STORY
Snow White's descendants were the first to feel the Queen's wrath. Believing the enchanted storybook to be a harmless family heirloom, a young mother read aloud the terrible tales writ upon its ancient pages.

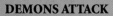

SHE IS THE WICKEDEST of witches, a sorceress from another dimension exiled to Earth as punishment for her great evils. Before science and fact overcame superstition and fear, the Queen menaced mankind with dragons and ogres and fairies. And then she met Snow White, a princess whose beauty surpassed the Queen's unearthly allure. The Queen's vanity sparked a war that killed thousands when her armies laid siege to Snow White's castle. But the princess was more crafty than her jealous foe, for she imprisoned the vicious Queen within an enchanted storybook. Unfortunately, the Queen of Fables thus became immortal!

FREE

DEMONS ATTACK
In a trice, the mother saw her boy transformed into a gingerbread boy! Goblins attacked them with gnashing teeth! And the Queen of Fables escaped her prison as the storybook unfurled in a whirlwind of peeling parchment!

Finally released from the enchanted storybook, the Queen of Fables wasted no time in seeking out the hated Snow White!

...INTO HER OVEN!"

Thanks to the Queen, the hungry witch who once lured Hansel and Gretel to her gingerbread house suddenly found Plastic Man and J'onn J'onzz just as appetizing!

THE ENCHANTED FOREST

The Queen of Fables awoke from her storybook slumber in 21st-century New York City and spied Snow White within a modern-day "crystal ball": television! Although the fair princess was long dead, the Queen mistook Wonder Woman as her ravishing rival Snow White while watching a TV news report. To trap the beautiful Amazon Princess of Themyscira, the Queen of Fables transformed New York into a dark, enchanted forest full of grim fairy-tale dangers.

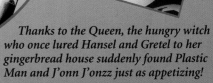

REAL NAME Unknown
OCCUPATION Sorceress
BASE Other-dimensional Space
HEIGHT Tall and willowy
WEIGHT Light as a feather
EYES Twin sapphires
HAIR Sleekest ebon
FIRST APPEARANCE
JLA #47
(November 2000)

NEVER NEVER LAND

Batman figured it out first. Though briefly expelled from the Justice League, the Dark Knight helped the JLA to understand the threat they faced, exposing the heroes to Snow White's enchanted storybook. Pulled into the realm of fantasy, the League learned that the Queen of Fables could turn classic fairy tales into reality, and make any legendary monster a tangible terror!

FACING THE TRUTH

To defeat the Queen of Fables, Wonder Woman had to prove that truth was stranger – and *stronger* – than fiction. While the male Justice Leaguers engaged the Queen's mythical monstrosities, Diana bound the Queen with her lasso and compelled the witch to see the truth.

BACK TO THE BOOK

Ensnared by Wonder Woman's golden lariat, the Queen came to a stunning realization: in the enchanted storybook, she was immortal. But in the real world she showed her true age. As the Queen withered into a desiccated hag, the Justice League imprisoned her upon the printed page once more. But this time they denied her the magic of fairyland by choosing a copy of the *United States Tax Code Manual*!

THE CRIME SYNDICATE

![JLA]

ON THE OTHER SIDE of a membrane separating the matter universe from its anti-matter reflection exists an Earth where wrong is right and darkness eclipses the light of good. Five super-humans rule this wicked world with evil hearts and iron fists. They are the Crime Syndicate of Amerika, whose Latin motto *Cui Bono* ("Who Profits?") epitomizes their lust for wealth and power. However the CSA met their match in the JLA, brought to this far-flung counterpart Earth by the heroic Alexander Luthor. Justice won out, but only briefly, for if such reversals were maintained, both universes would soon be destroyed!

OPPOSITES ATTRACT

The Crime Syndicate's roster includes Ultraman, Superwoman, Owlman, Power Ring, and Johnny Quick, immoral inverses of the JLA's Superman, Wonder Woman, Batman, Green Lantern, and the Flash. The JLA is bound by trust, the CSA have nothing but jealous enmity for one another (right).

THE PANOPTICON

Just like the JLA, the Crime Syndicate holds court on their Earth's Moon, in a fortress called the "Panopticon." The presence of statues to Dr. Noon, White Cat, Space Man, and other supervillains indicates that the CSA may have had other equally evil incarnations.

ALEXANDER LUTHOR

The Lex Luthor of the positive matter universe is dangerously depraved; however his anti-matter doppelganger is the model of angelic altruism. Unfortunately, the super-strong and supremely intelligent Alexander Luthor is also the lone heroic presence on his world and forever outnumbered five to one.

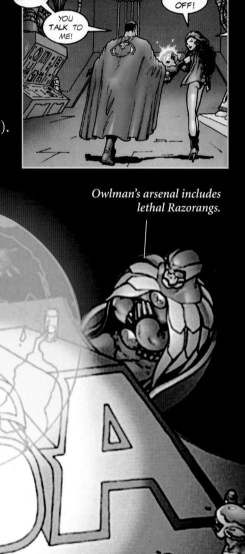

Ultraman replenishes his powers with exposure to Anti-Kryptonite.

Superwoman has great strength, a choking lariat, and laser-vision.

Owlman's arsenal includes lethal Razorangs.

Power Ring's emerald energies are fueled by the mystical entity Volthoom.

CARNAGE!

The JLA's plan was to hit the CSA hard and fast. After reversing through the dimensional membrane, Green Lantern trapped the Crime Syndicate in their lunar Panopticon beneath a pair of giant power ringed hands. Meanwhile, the remaining Justice League worked to free the anti-matter Earth. But all the Syndicate had to do was bide its time. Twenty-four hours after the League arrived, the CSA were transported to the matter universe Earth… now short one Justice League of America!

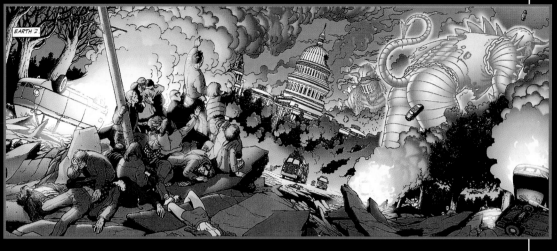

EXECUTIVE DECISION

Burning for payback, the Crime Syndicate vented their anger upon the Justice League's Earth. Washington, D.C., became a battleground, offering little resistance. As the world watched helplessly, Superwoman humiliated the President and readied him for execution on national television!

MARS ATTACKS!

Ultraman may have easily murdered the sole surviving White Martian on his world, but he never imagined his anti-world's positive matter counterpart would be so formidable an opponent. With the JLA caught unawares on the Syndicate's Earth, only J'onn J'onzz and Aquaman were left to quell the CSA's reign of destruction! To fell Ultraman, the Martian Manhunter morphed into a thorny nightmare long extinct on his native Red Planet!

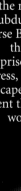

BRAINIAC ATTACK

As the JLA struggled to traverse the membrane once more and subdue the Syndicate, a parallel universe Brainiac added yet another threat to the equation. Long imprisoned in Ultraman's Flying Fortress, this evil organic syntellect escaped his isolation think-tank and sent the matter and anti-matter worlds on a collision course!

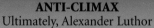

ULTRA-LOBOTOMY

The JLA realized too late that their attempts were in vain: nothing good could ever come of the anti-matter universe. However, the efforts of the JLA and the CSA saved their respective Earths from destruction and restored them to their proper places. Upon his return to the Flying Fortress, Ultraman seared off the lobe-buds of Brainiac's higher consciousness with a merciless beam of Ultra-Vision.

ANTI-CLIMAX

Ultimately, Alexander Luthor was once more left alone in the anti-matter universe to battle the Crime Syndicate. Across the dark mirror, evil prevailed. But the JLA had kindled an enduring spark of hope.

69

Techno-Tyrants

JLA

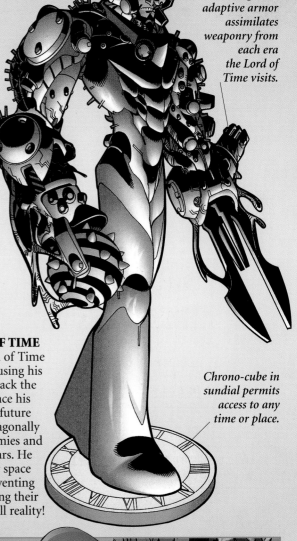

Temporal-adaptive armor assimilates weaponry from each era the Lord of Time visits.

Chrono-cube in sundial permits access to any time or place.

T HEY ARE ALL MISFITS and miscreants of science, industrious villains who misuse technology and invention for criminal acts. The Lord of Time and Solaris are man and machine respectively, each hailing from different disparate points in the far-off future. Conversely, the so-called Quantum Mechanics are Brobdingnagian beings birthed in the long ago "Big Bang" that created the known universe. Amazo and Tomorrow Woman are android antagonists, creations of archetypal mad scientists T. O. Morrow and Professor Ivo. The Ultramarines, meanwhile, are super-soldiers who chose to forsake their own humanity in order to become living weapons of mass destruction!

LORD OF TIME

From the year A.D. 3786, the Lord of Time attacked the Justice League, using his miraculous chrono-cube to peel back the fourth-dimensional veil of time. Since his initial defeat, this fugitive from the future has learned to move laterally and diagonally through history, accessing armies and armaments spanning millions of years. He wants nothing less than to conquer space and time, and is quite capable of preventing the JLA's origins by eliminating their ancestors in a bid to rule all reality!

SOLARIS
Like Hourman, the stellar supercomputer Solaris hails from the 853rd century. This man-made tyrant sun sought to conquer two eras! By encoding its evil in a techno-virus sent back to infect 20th-century machinery, Solaris literally created itself. The JLA and its future counterparts of Justice Legion-A had to join forces to defeat this sentient star.

I WILL NOT BE "HANDLED"

QUANTUM MECHANICS

On the eve of their demise, the immense Quantum Mechanics skewered hundreds of worlds – including Earth – from their natural orbits to create their own celestial ladder to Heaven. Realizing the Quantum Mechanics' goal was altruistic, albeit misguided, the JLA attempted to help them cross to a higher plane of existence, but found their mission thwarted by zealots within the Mechanics' own titanic populace!

AMAZO

He would be a one-man JLA if he were only human. Built by the insidious Professor Ivo (see below), the android Amazo was engineered specifically to aid Ivo's single-minded quest for immortality. Absorption cells in Amazo's body enabled the mechanical man to mimic the abilities of the original Justice League and every subsequent superhuman he encountered. Amazo's prime directive is to destroy the JLA. And with the powers of Aquaman, Black Canary, Flash, Green Lantern, and the Martian Manhunter replicated in his default mode, Amazo is frequently reactivated in various upgraded, virtually unstoppable forms.

THE ULTRAMARINES

General Wade Eiling initiated the "Ultramarines Project" to create meta-powered soldiers loyal to the U.S. Four Marine Corps officers were exposed to Proteum, an artificial isotope. Lt. Col. Scott Sawyer no longer has material substance, but inhabits the stealth weapon Warmaker One. Capt. Lea Corbin became the dimension-shifting 4-D. Maj. Dan Stone was transformed into the living liquid Flow. And Capt. John Wether utilizes the "unified field harmonic" to wield atomic powers as Pulse 8. Following Eiling's betrayal, the Ultramarines became the new "Global Guardians" of Superbia, a city-state floating high above the nuclear-ravaged ruins of Montevideo, Uruguay.

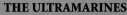

T. O. Morrow & Professor Ivo

A frequent foe of the JLA and JSA, scientific genius Thomas Oscar Morrow harbors a distinctly unhealthy obsession with the future, having invented the means to pluck technology from eras to come in order to plunder the present. Morrow's greatest creation may well be the Red Tornado, an android that turned on its creator to befriend his super-heroic foes. Ironically, Morrow's most recent human simulacrum, Tomorrow Woman, an android built with Professor Ivo, also proved to be more human than anticipated. After successfully joining the JLA, she too disobeyed her builders. She countermanded her programming to murder her new teammates, choosing to blow herself up instead!

Tomorrow Woman

71

IMMORTAL TERRORS
JLA

T**HESE AGELESS ANTAGONISTS** cheat the rigors of time, some even eluding death itself to fulfill their dark designs. Millennia ago, Vandal Savage went from caveman to conqueror simply by wishing on a fallen star. Neron may have been the first angel to fall from grace, plummeting from Heaven's splendor to lord over Hell's abyss. In his own realm, Qwsp could never tumble, for down and up have no meaning in the Fifth-Dimension. Dr. Destiny strikes through sleep, disrupting the dreams of others because of his own eternal exile from slumber. And Rama Khan vows to destroy anyone threatening to despoil his ancient paradise!

VANDAL SAVAGE

The last man of his kind on Earth, Vandar Adg of the Blood Tribe was a simple Cro-Magnon until exposure to the rays of a mysterious meteor evolved his intelligence and made him immortal. As Vandal Savage he has plotted to rule the Earth, even allying himself with the futuristic Solaris to achieve his goal.

SOULTAKER

A being of unimaginable power, Neron once boosted the metahuman abilities of the Justice League's most insidious foes. Many became barely recognizable monsters as Neron increased their capacities for evil in exchange for their already tarnished souls.

NERON

Satan. Beelzebub. Old Scratch. The Devil has many names, but each appellation pales next to the abominable Neron, whose hunger for human spirits is boundless. Neron delights in bargains and temptations, yearning to corrupt the incorruptible heroes of the JLA and prove that evil can triumph over good. However he has yet to enslave the World's Greatest Super Heroes.

Neron loosed two of the Demons Three – Abnegazar and Ghast – to tear the Moon from its orbit!

QWSP

Qwsp hails from fifth-dimensional Zrfff, where super-science mimics astounding magic. Years ago, "Quisp" (as he was then known) delighted in playing pranks on Aquaman. Eventually, the silver-haired sprite adopted a more malevolent mission, sparking a dimension-rattling war between the imps Lkz (an electrifying blue genie) and Johnny Thunder's pink "Thunderbolt" Yz. After his defeat by the combined JLA and JSA, Qwsp was remanded to Zrfff for suitable punishment.

DR DESTINY

His true identity a mystery, the cadaverous Dr. Destiny once constructed a machine that could make nightmares real. His "Materioptikon" – as Destiny dubbed it – was powered by a ruby talisman belonging to Morpheus, Lord of the Dreaming. It proved to have an unforeseen side effect on its inventor. Destiny's psyche-warping machine made him an insomniac and unable to dream; his body withered as his sleepless mind atrophied. Dr. Destiny has fantasies of destroying the JLA. Only then, he believes, will he rest easy.

In Dr. Destiny's nightmarish reality, Wonder Woman experienced the ravages of losing her immortality.

At one with the land of Jarhanpur, Rama Khan could call down lightning or torrents, command the vines and vegetation, or even rise up as a walking, stone-fisted mountain of malice!

RAMA KHAN

Since before recorded history, the nation of Jarhanpur was an oasis kept unsullied from foreign interlopers by the Rama Khan, a mortal guardian empowered by the land itself. When Wonder Woman sought to rescue an abducted boy chosen to succeed as Jarhanpur's ruler, the current Rama Khan met the visiting JLA in an elemental tumult. Truth itself broke down, threatening the Earth with utter catastrophe as Rama Khan broke Wonder Woman's supposedly unbreakable golden lasso. Ultimately, Wonder Woman restored the links of her lariat and the fundamental fabric of truth, reuniting mother and son in the process, but only by severing the bond between Rama Khan and Jarhanpur and leaving the land in ruins. For that, a vengeful Rama Khan has promised bloody vengeance on the Amazing Amazon and her fellow Justice Leaguers.

WITH ALL THE **FURY** A **MOTHER** CAN MUSTER.

YOU ARE AS INSECTS TO US HERE. YOUR OPINIONS. YOUR "MORALS." YOUR SO-CALLED STRENGTH...

INSIGNIFICANT AS **DUST** TO THE MOUNTAIN THAT IS **JARHANPUR.**

LEGACY OF THE LEAGUE

THE JUSTICE LEAGUE wasn't the first super-team. That distinction goes to the Justice Society of America, first chronicled by Gardner Fox – creator of the Flash, Hawkman, and Dr. Fate – in the winter of 1940, during what became known as comics' "Golden Age."

Readers' interest in costumed crime fighters gradually waned as comic books turned to other popular genres, such as westerns, romance, and science fiction. In time, DC Comics realized that the super hero archetype was due for revitalization.

So in early 1960, Fox joined with artist Mike Sekowsky to convene the first meeting of the Justice League of America. In less than a year, the JLA graduated to their very own comic book title. The JLA have since endured through more than 600 adventures published over four decades. The membership of the League may change, but "The World's Greatest Heroes" – as they were dubbed in their very first cover blurb – continue to fight the good fight and uphold justice in the grandest of traditions.

THE JUSTICE LEAGUES

JLA

ONE TEAM, MANY HEROES. The Justice League of America began with five founding members banding together to battle invading aliens from the planet Appellax. But when the Appellaxians were abducted by a clandestine organization known only as "Locus," Black Canary, Aquaman, The Flash, Green Lantern, and the Martian Manhunter voted to remain a team… at least until the mystery of Locus was solved. Fortunately, the JLA lasted far beyond that, swelling in ranks, disbanding more than once, but nevertheless enduring in concept and spirit through countless triumphs and tragedies.

STRENGTH IN NUMBERS

Next came the Atom. Then Green Arrow and Hawkman. Superman and Batman initially opted for reserve status, but joined the team more often than not. However, Metamorpho declined, as did The Phantom Stranger, who was named an "honorary member." In time, the JLA roster would include Red Tornado, Elongated Man, Hawkgirl, Zatanna, and Firestorm!

THE FOUNDING FIVE

To ready their secret society for an anticipated apocalypse, Locus experimented on the Appellaxians, who were in turn secretly manipulating Locus to learn the secrets of Earth's metahuman heroes. One by one, the costumed champions fell, leaving only the newly formed JLA to repel an all-out alien invasion!

FALLEN HEROES

With the JLA's ranks stretched thin and its satellite destroyed by a scattering of aliens known as "The Debris," Aquaman dissolved the League and assembled a more streamlined team. J'onn J'onzz, Elongated Man, and Zatanna remained, soon joined by the cyborg Steel, seismic-rumbling Vibe, camouflaging Gypsy, and animal-powered Vixen. Unfortunately, this group was short-lived, disbanding after Professor Ivo's androids murdered Vibe and Steel.

JUSTICE LEAGUE

Darkseid called it "Operation: Humiliation" when the acid-tongued Glorious Godfrey stirred human against metahuman as Parademon and Warhound hordes attacked Earth! But the Lord of Apokolips only strengthened the legendary heroes' resolve, and when the dust settled a grateful mankind welcomed Batman, Mister Miracle and his assistant Oberon, Black Canary, Dr. Fate, Captain Marvel, J'onn J'onzz, Blue Beetle, and Dr. Light as the all-new Justice League!

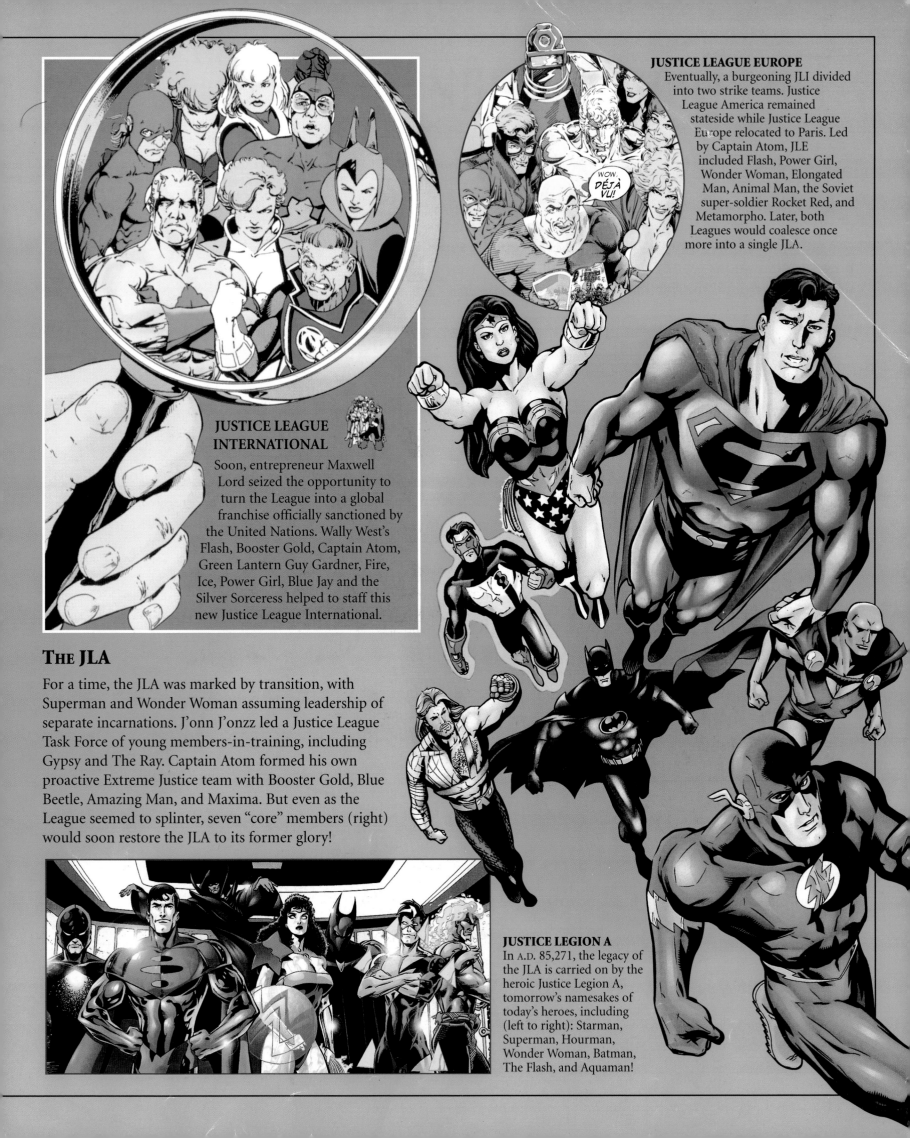

JUSTICE LEAGUE INTERNATIONAL

Soon, entrepreneur Maxwell Lord seized the opportunity to turn the League into a global franchise officially sanctioned by the United Nations. Wally West's Flash, Booster Gold, Captain Atom, Green Lantern Guy Gardner, Fire, Ice, Power Girl, Blue Jay and the Silver Sorceress helped to staff this new Justice League International.

THE JLA

For a time, the JLA was marked by transition, with Superman and Wonder Woman assuming leadership of separate incarnations. J'onn J'onzz led a Justice League Task Force of young members-in-training, including Gypsy and The Ray. Captain Atom formed his own proactive Extreme Justice team with Booster Gold, Blue Beetle, Amazing Man, and Maxima. But even as the League seemed to splinter, seven "core" members (right) would soon restore the JLA to its former glory!

JUSTICE LEAGUE EUROPE

Eventually, a burgeoning JLI divided into two strike teams. Justice League America remained stateside while Justice League Europe relocated to Paris. Led by Captain Atom, JLE included Flash, Power Girl, Wonder Woman, Elongated Man, Animal Man, the Soviet super-soldier Rocket Red, and Metamorpho. Later, both Leagues would coalesce once more into a single JLA.

WOW, DÉJÀ VU!

JUSTICE LEGION A

In A.D. 85,271, the legacy of the JLA is carried on by the heroic Justice Legion A, tomorrow's namesakes of today's heroes, including (left to right): Starman, Superman, Hourman, Wonder Woman, Batman, The Flash, and Aquaman!

THE TROPHY ROOM

As its CURATOR Zauriel once argued, the JLA's Trophy Room symbolizes *vigilance*, not violence. The mementos on display in this special wing of the Watchtower represent the enormity of evil the team has faced, and celebrate the super-powered champions – both living and dead – who have risked their lives to defend the Earth.

1 Z'ONN Z'ORR GLOBE Model reveals the White Martians' planned realignment of Earth's continents.

2 I.F. The "Implicate Field" is a 32nd-century quantum technology weapon confiscated from the Lord of Time.

3 THE KEY'S KEY-RING A sample of the villain's skeleton keys and psychotropic chemical injectors.

4 THE ROYAL FLUSH GANG Oversized playing cards replicate a two-dimensional trap once holding the Gang's Ten, Hi-Jack, Queen, King, and Ace .

5 SOLARIS Illuminating facsimile of the 853rd-century tyrant sun, a super-computer defeated by the JLA and Justice Legion A.

6 PIRANHA PENGUINS Justice League Antarctica encountered Adélie penguins bioengineered to have the teeth and voraciousness of Amazonian piranha.

7 TRAUMIEL'S ASHES Remains of the angel loyal to Asmodel who was disintegrated by Zauriel's sonic scream are mounted on canvas with runes etched by Zauriel to describe the event.

8 ENGINE OF CHANCE Deceased quantum physicist Julian September's probability-altering machine, capable of re-ordering reality by a factor of "lucky" seven.

9 KIRBY DOTS Bits of "dark matter" sealed in a vacuum chamber pending study.

10 ARTIFICIAL KRYPTONITE Radiation-depleted isotope of the rare element.

11 THE BUG Miniature model of Blue Beetle's scarab-shaped hover-ship.

12 WORLOGOG Kyle Rayner's sculpted interpretation of the "Philosopher's Stone" – the reality-altering Worlogog that Lex Luthor wielded against the JLA.

13 PARADEMON ARMOR Headpiece worn by Darkseid's elite flying stormtroopers.

14 PROMETHEUS' HELMET The murderous mastermind's computerized helmet was scuttled by Batman after downloading its wealth of information onto JLA archive servers.

15 AMAZO'S HEAD Deactivated central processing unit from one of the android's early prototype bodies.

16 THE RAY'S CRASH HELMET Spare helmet worn by Ray Terrill (The Ray), briefly a member of the Justice League Task Force before joining Young Justice.

17 LITTLE LEAGUERS Malicious micro-robot duplicates of the Justice League built by the Toyman and Abra Kadabra.

18 BRAIN STORM'S THINKING CAP This channels stellar energy to boost intelligence, animates objects, enables its wearer to hurl "star-bolts," and permits teleportation.

19 STARRO PROBE Stasis tank keeps the Star Conqueror's face-hugging mental probe inert. Occasional feeding is required.

20 POWER BATTERY Replica of original Green Lantern Alan Scott's emerald power battery, carved from the meteoric Starheart, repository of the universe's random magicks.

21 TRIUMPH The Justice League's "lost" founding member Will McIntyre (Triumph) is forever frozen, transformed into a statue of ice for his treachery by the Spectre. Cooling units keep sublimation to a minimum, should the Spirit of Wrath choose to offer McIntyre a reprieve.

22 TRICK ARROWS A sample of Green Arrow Oliver Queen's shafts.

23 PORTRAIT GALLERY Holographic bank depicts constantly rotating assemblage of every JLA hero and heroine.

24 GAMMA GONG Dhorian dictator Kanjar Ro's paralyzing weapon. When struck, the Gong incapacitates anyone in its vicinity.

25 SUPERMAN-ROBOT COSTUME Uniform worn by one of the robotic Men of Steel created by Superman to police the Earth.

26 BATARANGS Working samples of Batman's signature weapon.

27 BLUE BEETLE'S WEAPONRY Compressed air-firing B.B. Gun; replica of first Beetle Dan Garrett's mystical scarab; hand-held remote for the high-flying Bug.

28 WANDJINA'S LABYRIS Battleaxe belonging to "The Thunderer," a parallel dimension hero who perished stopping a Russian nuclear reactor meltdown after attempting to rid the communist nation of its deadly atomic arsenal.

29 AZTEK'S HELM The late Justice Leaguer's sun-motif helmet was the source of his 4-dimensional powers. It remains in JLA possession pending a custody battle initiated by Aztek's former benefactors, the Q Foundation.

30 MARTIAN JUMP-SHIP Unaltered model of the Martian shuttle, seen here in its primary configuration.

31 KEY-MEN The Key's helper automatons with their clockwork motivators safely removed.

32 S.T.A.R. LABS SHUTTLE Scale model of a prototype spacecraft rescued by the JLA.

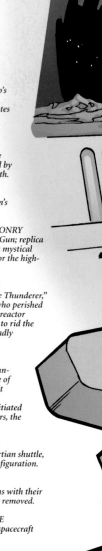

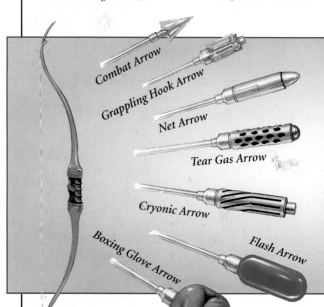

Combat Arrow

Grappling Hook Arrow

Net Arrow

Tear Gas Arrow

Cryonic Arrow

Boxing Glove Arrow

Flash Arrow

GREEN ARROW'S TRICK ARROWS

The Combat Arrow features a razor-sharp titanium broadhead blade. The Grappling Hook Arrow contains coiled rappelling cord in its hollow shaft. The Net Arrow unfurls a nylon mesh upon impact. The Tear Gas Arrow distributes incapacitating CS gas. The Cryonic Arrow contains compartments of Helipolysulficate and Restifreeze, chemicals that combine on impact to encase a target in a sheath of ice. The Flash Arrow features a quick-burning magnesium flare. The Boxing Glove Arrow, meanwhile, may look unwieldy, but delivers a knockout punch.

This is just one wing of the Trophy Room, which houses hundreds of items, both real memorabilia and faithfully recreated facsimiles relating to the Justice League's cases. More dangerous items are stored in vaults accessible only to core JLA members.

JLA TIMELINE

The Justice Society (left to right): The Atom, Sandman, The Spectre, Flash, Hawkman, Dr. Fate, Green Lantern, and Hourman.

OVER 40 YEARS OLD and showing very little wear, the JLA continues a rich tradition inaugurated by DC Comics' Justice Society of America. Beginning in 1960, five of the World's Greatest Super Heroes rekindled the spark of super-team action, acknowledging that justice stands strongest when it stands together!

THE BRAVE and the BOLD presents MAR. NO. 28

JUSTICE LEAGUE of AMERICA

THE WORLD'S GREATEST HEROES TEAM UP TO BATTLE

"STARRO THE CONQUEROR!"

10¢

Upon its arrival on Earth, Starro enlisted three starfish "distant relatives" for planetary conquest. To defeat Starro, the JLA encased the nuclear-powered alien in quicklime!

1940

Winter: The JLA's inspiration, **The Justice Society of America**, unites in the pages of ALL-STAR COMICS #3!

1960

February–March: **The Justice League of America** first appear with **Wonder Woman, The Flash, Aquaman, Green Lantern,** and the **Martian Manhunter** teaming to spare the denizens of Happy Harbor, Rhode Island, from the mental thrall of **Starro the Conqueror**! **Superman** and **Batman** are revealed as fellow JLA members, although they do not aid in the adventure. "Young hipster" **Lucas "Snapper" Carr** is made an honorary member of the JLA and becomes the team's official "mascot." The Secret Sanctuary, a mountain cavern outside of Happy Harbor, is established as the League's first headquarters. (THE BRAVE AND THE BOLD #28)

April–May: In its second appearance, the JLA battles **Xotar the Weapons Master**, a fiend from the future! (THE BRAVE AND THE BOLD #29)

Elsewhere, **Ralph Dibny**, the stretchable sleuth known as **The Elongated Man**, first appears. (THE FLASH vol. 1 #112)

June–July: The JLA meets **Professor Ivo** and his android **Amazo**, an automaton with all the super powers of the Justice League members! (THE BRAVE AND THE BOLD #30)

Also, the reincarnating villain **Duncan Pramble**, a.k.a. **Multi-Man**, debuts in the pages of CHALLENGERS OF THE UNKNOWN #14.

August: **The Tornado Tyrant,** later the sentient spirit of **Red Tornado,** first appears on the planet Rann. (MYSTERY IN SPACE #61)

Elsewhere, the criminal **Clock King** first appears. (WORLD'S FINEST COMICS #111)

October–November: The JLA graduates to its own comic book title, in time to play a deadly game of chess with the three-eyed Kalanorian tyrant **Despero**! The Leaguers lose and are teleported to strange planets. (JUSTICE LEAGUE OF AMERICA #1)

1961

February–March: The JLA battles evil alien despots **Hyathis**, Queen of planet Alstair, and **Kanjar Ro**, dictator of planet Dhor, who paralyzes Earth's population with his Gamma Gong. (JUSTICE LEAGUE OF AMERICA #3)

Elsewhere, Thanagarian policeman **Katar Hol** becomes Earth's second **Hawkman**! **Shayera Thal** is introduced as the second **Hawkgirl** (later Hawkwoman). (THE BRAVE AND THE BOLD #34)

April–May: Playboy **Oliver Queen**, a.k.a. **Green Arrow**, is elected the sixth member of the JLA. He is then kidnapped by the warlord Carthan of the planet Dryanna. (JUSTICE LEAGUE OF AMERICA #4)

June–July: The deadly dream-warping **Dr. Destiny** debuts in the pages of JUSTICE LEAGUE OF AMERICA #5.

Elsewhere, **The Shadow Thief** first appears. (THE BRAVE AND THE BOLD #36)

August–September: The JLA first encounters that diabolical manipulator of chance **Professor Amos Fortune.** (JUSTICE LEAGUE OF AMERICA #6)

JUSTICE LEAGUE of AMERICA

"The WHEEL of MISFORTUNE"

Amos Fortune's "Wheel of Misfortune" eliminated the Justice Leaguers' "good-luck glands" by firing a charge into them when they passed its pointer!

Dr. Arthur Light claimed to have mastered all the secrets of light, revealing powers that would enable him to take over the world! But first he had to eliminate the JLA!

The Crime Syndicate of America
The villains of Earth-3's Crime Syndicate crossed the dimensional barrier and invaded Earth-1. The Syndicate realized that one-on-one battles with their heroic opposites in the Justice League would end in stalemates, so most took on different opponents!

Superwoman bound Wonder Woman with her own unbreakable lasso!

A super-strong tap from the evil Ultraman sent the Flash tumbling!

With the radiating light of his Illumina-Gun, Owlman zapped Green Lantern unconscious!

A dizzying dervish courtesy of Johnny Quick spun Batman senseless!

Power Ring subdued the Man of Steel in a magical emerald snare!

September–October: Physicist **Ray Palmer** uses the fragment of a white dwarf star to shrink himself into the mighty mite known as **The Atom!** (SHOWCASE #34)

1962
February: Readers discover the "origin" of the JLA, which is revealed in flashback as the World's Greatest Super Heroes band together to defeat seven bizarre aliens from the planet Appellax: **Golden Roc, Diamond Man, Fire Giant, Wood King, Stone God, Glass Man**, and a **Mercury Blob!** (JUSTICE LEAGUE OF AMERICA #9)

March: The JLA battles sinister sorcerer **Felix Faust** and the four-dimensional **Lord of Time**, as well as the **Demons Three: Abnegazar, Rath,** and **Ghast!** (JUSTICE LEAGUE OF AMERICA #10)

June: **Dr. Light** debuts, adding another scientific menace to the JLA's rogues gallery. (JUSTICE LEAGUE OF AMERICA #12)

September: The Atom joins the JLA as its seventh official member. But under the influence of **Mr. Memory**, the other League members can't remember who the Atom is – or why they ever elected him! (JUSTICE LEAGUE OF AMERICA #14)

1963
February: The evil Tornado Tyrant becomes a good **Tornado Champion**, battling the JLA in order to devise a means to defeat its own menacing cyclone clone. (JUSTICE LEAGUE OF AMERICA #17)

August: The JLA meets the Justice Society of America, heroes of Earth-2 and DC Comics' "Golden Age," as both groups begin the first of their annual team-ups, this time to defeat villains

Green Lantern and the rest of the JLA learned too late that a blast of the Key's psycho-chemicals would turn super heroes into super-slaves!

from two worlds: **The Wizard, Icicle, The Fiddler,** Felix Faust, **Chronos**, and **Dr. Alchemy!** (JUSTICE LEAGUE OF AMERICA #21)

November: **The Queen Bee** first stings the JLA. (JUSTICE LEAGUE OF AMERICA #23)

1964
June–July: With their Justice League mentors as inspiration, **Robin, Aqualad**, and **Kid Flash** join forces as **The Teen Titans.** (THE BRAVE AND THE BOLD #54)

August and September: The JLA and JSA meet and battle the evil **Crime Syndicate** (**Ultraman, Superwoman, Johnny Quick, Power Ring**, and **Owlman**) of Earth-3! (JUSTICE LEAGUE OF AMERICA #29–30)

October–November: **Zatanna Zatara** is introduced in the pages of HAWKMAN vol. 1 #4.

November: The high-flying Hawkman becomes the eighth member of the JLA. (JUSTICE LEAGUE OF AMERICA #31)

December: The JLA first battles the criminal scientist **Axel Storm**, better known as the thinking cap-wearing **Brain Storm!** (JUSTICE LEAGUE OF AMERICA #32)

December 1964–January 1965: Soldier-of-fortune and world-famous adventurer **Rex Mason** is

transformed into the elemental freak **Metamorpho!** (THE BRAVE AND THE BOLD #57)

1965
February: The JLA battles the **Alien-ator**, a futuristic foe who transforms the League members into alien-like beings! (JUSTICE LEAGUE OF AMERICA #33)

August and September: When **Johnny Thunder**'s evil Earth-1 counterpart seizes control of the magical **Thunderbolt** and journeys back in time to prevent the origins of the JLA's membership, the JSA is forced to battle the **Lawless League of Earth-A** in this reality-altering JLA/JSA team-up adventure. (JUSTICE LEAGUE OF AMERICA #37–38)

December: **The Key** and his **Key-Men** debut in "The Key-Master of the World!" (JUSTICE LEAGUE OF AMERICA #41)

1966
February: In "Metamorpho Says No!" the Element Man opts not to join the JLA. (JUSTICE LEAGUE OF AMERICA #42)

March: The JLA is dealt a deadly hand when Amos Fortune's **Royal Flush Gang** (Amos Fortune/Ace, King, Queen, Jack, and Ten) attacks in spades! (JUSTICE LEAGUE OF AMERICA #43)

June: The JLA meets two unstoppable monsters when **Prof. Andrew Zagarian** creates **Shaggy Man** and **Shaggy Man II**! (JUSTICE LEAGUE OF AMERICA #45)

August and September: "To touch **Anti-Matter Man** was to reach instant destruction!" Worlds collide as the Anti-Matter Man wreaks a "Crisis Between Earth-1 and Earth-2!" in the fourth annual JLA/JSA crossover. (JUSTICE LEAGUE OF AMERICA #46–47)

November: **Blue Beetle** Ted Kord debuts in the pages of Charlton Comics' CAPTAIN ATOM vol. 1 #83!

1967
February: Zatanna and The Elongated Man guest in JUSTICE LEAGUE OF AMERICA #51, which reunites the Mistress of Magic with her long-lost father **John Zatara**!

March: In "Missing in Action – 5 Justice Leaguers," Snapper Carr reveals why the entire JLA roster isn't involved in every chronicled adventure. (JUSTICE LEAGUE OF AMERICA #52)

August and September: In "The Super-Crisis That Struck Earth-Two," an adult Robin from Earth-2 helps the Justice Society and the Justice League battle the other-dimensional **Black Spheres**! (JUSTICE LEAGUE OF AMERICA #55–56)

1968

March: In the event of Hal Jordan's incapacitation, fellow Earthman **Guy Gardner** is selected to be alternate Green Lantern of Space Sector 2814. (GREEN LANTERN vol. 2 #59)

August: T. O. Morrow's android hero Red Tornado makes his first official appearance in an adventure featuring only the Justice Society of America. The JLA is absent from its own comic book! (JUSTICE LEAGUE OF AMERICA #64)

1969

February: Wonder Woman becomes the first member to resign from the JLA! (JUSTICE LEAGUE OF AMERICA #69)

March: At Batman's urging, the JLA checks up on the costumed adventurer and guest-star **The Creeper**. (JUSTICE LEAGUE OF AMERICA #70)

May: J'onn J'onzz resigns his membership, exiting the Justice League and journeying into space with his fellow Martians to find a new Martian homeworld. (JUSTICE LEAGUE OF AMERICA #71)

September: Following the death of her husband (private detective **Larry Lance**, who was killed by the insane

After Wonder Woman, Black Canary was the second female member of the Justice Society and its Earth-1 counterpart, the Justice League!

living star **Aquarius**) the grieving Earth-2 heroine **Black Canary** journeys to Earth-1 to make a new life for herself. (JUSTICE LEAGUE OF AMERICA #74)

November: Black Canary officially joins the JLA. (JUSTICE LEAGUE OF AMERICA #75)

December: Snapper Carr unwittingly aids "Mr. Average" **John Dough** (in reality, **The Joker**), turning the public against the JLA and revealing the location of the Secret Sanctuary in the process! (JUSTICE LEAGUE OF AMERICA #77)

1970

February: With its Secret Sanctuary compromised, the Justice League relocates to the **JLA Satellite**, an orbiting headquarters 22,300 miles above the Earth, accessible only via a

Thanagarian relativity-beam teleport device. Also, the League is aided by **The Vigilante** (a.k.a. **Greg Sanders**) in defeating the alien Doomsters. (JUSTICE LEAGUE OF AMERICA #78)

August and September: The JLA and JSA battle to prevent **Creator²**, an alien contractor determined to destroy Earth-1 and Earth-2 in a cosmic collision. (JUSTICE LEAGUE OF AMERICA #82–83)

1971

February: The JLA meets **Blue Jay**, **Wandjina**, **Jack B. Quick**, and **Silver Sorceress**, heroes of the doomed planet Angor. (JUSTICE LEAGUE OF AMERICA #87)

February–March: The "Dog of War" **Orion** first appears in the pages of NEW GODS vol. 1 #1. Fellow New Gods **Lightray** and **Metron** also make their debuts here.

August and September: The JLA and the JSA join forces to reunite the alien boy **A-Rym** with his pet **Tippy** before each perishes in this crossover, which pits both teams against the evil powerhouse **Solomon Grundy**! (JUSTICE LEAGUE OF AMERICA #91–92)

September–October: Female Fury (and later *Mrs.* Mr. Miracle) **Big Barda** is introduced. (MISTER MIRACLE vol. 1 #4)

The Tornado Champion saved the JLA from the Tornado Tyrant's wicked whirlwinds by mentally creating an illusory rescue plane to vacuum the Leaguers to safety!

How do you defeat the undefeatable? After turning the Shaggy Man upon the unstoppable Moon-Being, the League buried them both underground… with another Shaggy Man! When the Shaggy Men overcame the Moon-Being, they would spend eternity fighting one another, or so the JLA hoped!

November: The rogue archer and **League of Assassins** member **Merlyn** makes his debut in this adventure, which also features the immortal spirit **Deadman,** who was formerly a murdered circus aerialist named Boston Brand! (JUSTICE LEAGUE OF AMERICA #94)

December: The Metropolis-based research facility **S.T.A.R. Labs,** which will prove both a boon and bane to the JLA in later years, is introduced. (SUPERMAN vol. 1 #246)

1972

February: The JLA battles **Starbreaker,** a cosmic vampire threatening Adam Strange's adopted Rann! (JUSTICE LEAGUE OF AMERICA #96)

May: **Sargon the Sorcerer** – the possessor of the mystical Ruby of Life – aids the JLA's defeat of Starbreaker. (JUSTICE LEAGUE OF AMERICA #98)

After the element man Metamorpho, the enigmatic Phantom Stranger was the second super hero to decline JLA membership.

August through October: The JLA travels through time with the JSA to rescue **The Seven Soldiers of Victory** (Vigilante, Green Arrow, **Speedy, Star-Spangled Kid, Stripesy, Shining Knight,** and the **Crimson Avenger**) and defeat the **Iron Hand.** Like the Crimson Avenger's sidekick, **Wing,** Red Tornado gives his life to defeat **The Nebula Man.** (JUSTICE LEAGUE OF AMERICA #100–102)

December: **The Phantom Stranger** is elected to JLA membership, but disappears before his induction ceremony. (JUSTICE LEAGUE OF AMERICA #103)

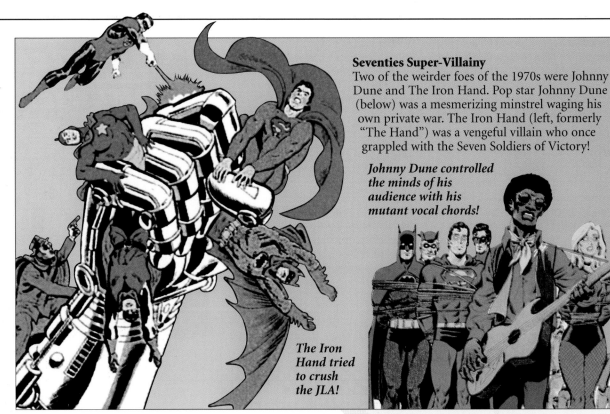

Seventies Super-Villainy
Two of the weirder foes of the 1970s were Johnny Dune and The Iron Hand. Pop star Johnny Dune (below) was a mesmerizing minstrel waging his own private war. The Iron Hand (left, formerly "The Hand") was a vengeful villain who once grappled with the Seven Soldiers of Victory!

Johnny Dune controlled the minds of his audience with his mutant vocal chords!

The Iron Hand tried to crush the JLA!

1973

May: Elongated Man is awarded JLA membership! (JUSTICE LEAGUE OF AMERICA #105)

June: The android Red Tornado, believed destroyed, returns to join the JLA! (JUSTICE LEAGUE OF AMERICA #106)

September–October and November–December: In their annual crossover, the JLA and JSA discover Earth-X, a Nazi-overrun alternate world and home to the heroic **Freedom Fighters** (**Uncle Sam, Phantom Lady, Doll Man, The Human Bomb, Black Condor,** and **The Ray**), a super-team debuting here. (JUSTICE LEAGUE OF AMERICA #107–108)

1974

January–February: Hawkman resigns from the JLA, but not before coming to the League's assistance as it battles **Eclipso**! (JUSTICE LEAGUE OF AMERICA #109)

March–April: With **Hal Jordan** incapacitated, **John Stewart** takes on the mantle of Green Lantern to aid the JLA in defeating the Key in "The Man Who Murdered Santa Claus." This holiday tale ends with a special Christmas gift for Red Tornado: a new costume! (JUSTICE LEAGUE OF AMERICA #110)

May–June: The mysterious villain known as **Libra** organizes the first **Injustice Gang of the World,** with membership including **The Tattooed Man,** Shadow Thief, **Chronos,**

Poison Ivy, Mirror Master, and the **Scarecrow.** (JUSTICE LEAGUE OF AMERICA #111)

September–October: In a one-issue crossover, the JLA and JSA join forces to battle a giant sand creature revealed to be **Sandy the Golden Boy,** once the teen sidekick of the Justice Society's **Wesley Dodds** (a.k.a. **The Sandman**). (JUSTICE LEAGUE OF AMERICA #113)

1975

January–February: J'onn J'onzz returns to enlist the JLA's help in defeating the alien deity **Korge,** although the Martian Manhunter does not resume League membership at this time. (JUSTICE LEAGUE OF AMERICA #115)

April: Hawkman returns and rejoins the JLA. (JUSTICE LEAGUE OF AMERICA #117)

August: After Kanjar Ro's defeat, the JLA are guests at the wedding of **Adam Strange** and his beloved **Alanna.** (JUSTICE LEAGUE OF AMERICA #121)

A teleporter mishap merges the alien Dharlu with the bodies of Hawkman and the Flash in JUSTICE LEAGUE OF AMERICA #130

Elsewhere, **The Manhunters** – renegade android enforcers created by the **Guardians of the Universe** – and their cunning Earthly agent **Mark Shaw** first appear. (FIRST ISSUE SPECIAL #5)

September: In "The Great Identity Crisis," an untold tale from the JLA's early adventures, the team members reveal their secret identities to one another. (JUSTICE LEAGUE OF AMERICA #122)

October and November: The JLA and JSA unite to defeat Earth-2's **Injustice Society** (The Wizard, Icicle, **Sportsmaster, Huntress, Shade,** and **The Gambler**) in the evil team's first modern-day appearance. (JUSTICE LEAGUE OF AMERICA #123–124)

1976

February: Wonder Woman officially rejoins the JLA. (JUSTICE LEAGUE OF AMERICA #127)

May–June: **The Secret Society of Super-Villains** debuts as Manhunter **Paul Kirk** assembles **Copperhead, Sinestro, Captain Boomerang,** Shadow Thief, Mirror Master, **Hi-Jack, Gorilla Grodd, Captain Cold,** and **Star Sapphire II** to thwart Darkseid's takeover of Earth. Later, the team frequently battles the JLA. (SECRET SOCIETY OF SUPER-VILLAINS #1)

October through December: The heroes of three worlds join forces to prevent an all-new crisis as the JLA and JSA unite with Earth-S's **Marvel Family** (**Captain Marvel**, **Mary Marvel**, and **Captain Marvel, Jr.**), **Bulletman**, **Bulletgirl**, **Ibis the Invincible**, **Mr. Scarlet**, **Pinky**, and **Spy Smasher**! (JUSTICE LEAGUE OF AMERICA #135–137

1977

March: The JLA first encounters the rogue android Manhunters and their **Grandmaster**. (JUSTICE LEAGUE OF AMERICA #140)

Also this month, physicist Martin Stein and high-school student Ronnie Raymond are atomically fused into the flame-haired **Firestorm**! (FIRESTORM #1)

April: Teacher Jefferson Pierce becomes the super-charged **Black Lightning** to fight street crime in Metropolis's embattled Suicide Slum. (BLACK LIGHTNING #1)

May: The JLA first battles **The Construct.** (JUSTICE LEAGUE OF AMERICA #142)

June: **The Privateer** attacks the League. (JUSTICE LEAGUE OF AMERICA #143)

July: The JLA's true origin is revealed in a flashback tale guest-starring TV Detective **Roy Raymond**, the **Blackhawks**, Robin, **Plastic Man**, **Congo Bill** and **Congorilla**, **Robotman**, Vigilante, **Rex the Wonder Dog**, and **The Challengers of the Unknown**. (JUSTICE LEAGUE OF AMERICA #144)

September: After aiding the JLA on so many occasions, Hawkgirl finally joins the team officially. (JUSTICE LEAGUE OF AMERICA #146)

October: Australia's **Tasmanian Devil** – here a Global Guardian and later a JLI member – first appears in the pages of SUPER FRIENDS #7 alongside future Justice League Task Force members **Zan** and **Jayna**, the **Wonder Twins**!

October and November: The JLA and JSA team with the 30th century's Legion of Super-Heroes to defeat **Mordru, Psycho-Pirate II**, and the Demons Three. (JUSTICE LEAGUE OF AMERICA #147–148)

December: The JLA first battles the **Star-Tsar**, revealed to be the League's former mascot Snapper Carr, in thrall to the *real* Star-Tsar, Mark Shaw. (JUSTICE LEAGUE OF AMERICA #149)

Also this month, future Justice League America member **Icemaiden** (Sigrid Nansen) first appears. (SUPER FRIENDS #9)

1978

January: The sesquicentennial JUSTICE LEAGUE OF AMERICA #150 sees the return of the Key as Snapper Carr redeems himself for his earlier betrayal by helping the League to defeat **The Star-Lords!**

April: The JLA grapples with the misguided **Ultraa**, a super hero of the alternate world known as Earth-Prime. (JUSTICE LEAGUE OF AMERICA #153)

October and November: To stop the Lord of Time, the JLA and JSA must team with five heroes from the past: **Jonah Hex**, **Viking Prince**, **Enemy Ace**, **Miss Liberty**, and **Black Pirate**! (JUSTICE LEAGUE OF AMERICA #159–160)

December: Zatanna finally joins the JLA! (JUSTICE LEAGUE OF AMERICA #161)

1979

May through July: JLA members Superman, Batman, Wonder Woman, Zatanna, and Green Lantern find themselves trapped within the bodies of The Secret Society of Super-Villains' Wizard **Blockbuster**, **Floronic Man**, **Star Sapphire**, and **Reverse-Flash**, respectively. (JUSTICE LEAGUE OF AMERICA #166–168)

October: The annual JLA/JSA crossover begins in tragedy as the two teams race to reveal "Who Killed Mr. Terrific?" (JUSTICE LEAGUE OF AMERICA #171–172)

Elsewhere, the Global Guardian known as the **Green Flame** (later the JLI's **Fire**) first appears. (SUPER FRIENDS #25)

December: Black Lightning first declines JLA membership. (JUSTICE LEAGUE OF AMERICA #173)

1980

January: In the concluding chapter of a two-part team-up, Black Lightning once more turns down a seat in the Justice League. (JUSTICE LEAGUE OF AMERICA #174)

June: Firestorm becomes a member of the JLA. (JUSTICE LEAGUE OF AMERICA #179)

August: Green Arrow resigns from the JLA after the team battles Star Tsar II. (JUSTICE LEAGUE OF AMERICA #181)

Zatanna never had her own regular title, although she did merit an occasional special and miniseries.

The JLA thwarted a robotic servant of alien parasite Nekron in JUSTICE LEAGUE OF AMERICA #128–129.

The Fourth World's New Gods joined the fray during the annual JLA/JSA crossover, this time marking the Justice League's initial full-length encounter with Darkseid!

October through December: In this year's crossover, the JLA and JSA battle the Injustice Society and the forces of Darkseid on Apokolips! (JUSTICE LEAGUE OF AMERICA #183–185)

1981

July: **The Vixen** makes her very first appearance in the pages of this month's ACTION COMICS #521.

October through December: **The Ultra-Humanite** – now in the body of a mutated albino ape – recruits villains from two Earths as the JLA and JSA face off against a newer and deadlier Secret Society of Super-Villains (**UH, The Mist, Cheetah, Killer Frost, Rag Doll,** Floronic Man, **Brainwave, Psycho-Pirate, Signalman,** and **The Monocle**). (JUSTICE LEAGUE OF AMERICA #195–197)

The Ultra-Humanite was Superman's very first supervillain foe, a mad scientist with a penchant for transplanting his brain into other bodies!

1982

March: Green Arrow rejoins the JLA in time to aid his teammates battle the Appellaxian aliens once more in this celebratory 72-page giant bicentennial issue! (JUSTICE LEAGUE OF AMERICA #200)

October through December: Earth-2's militant **Per Degaton** and Earth-3's Crime Syndicate are the threats behind "Crisis on Earth-Prime," the latest JLA/JSA thriller, guest-starring the World War II-era **All-Star Squadron** (**Robotman, Liberty Belle, Steel, Firebrand,** and **Johnny Quick**). (JUSTICE LEAGUE OF AMERICA #207–209)

1983

January through March: It's never too late for a great JLA adventure as a story intended for an oversized 1977 DC tabloid edition is finally published. (JUSTICE LEAGUE OF AMERICA #210–212)

September: **Albert Rothstein** becomes second-generation super hero **Nuklon. Todd Rice** establishes himself as fellow defender **Obsidian.** Both join sons and daughters of the JSA to form **Infinity Inc.** (ALL-STAR SQUADRON #25)

October and November: The JLA and JSA join together once again to defeat the **Johnny Thunder of Earth-1** in an adventure revealing that Black Canary was actually the daughter of Earth-2's Black Canary. (JUSTICE LEAGUE OF AMERICA #219–220)

1984

March: Infinity Inc. – a team featuring future members of both the JLA and JSA – graduates to its own series, which lasts 53 issues, two annuals, and one special! (INFINITY INC. #1)

July: J'onn J'onzz returns to the JLA as Martians invade Earth. (JUSTICE LEAGUE OF AMERICA #228)

October: Aquaman convenes a new JLA lineup, including veterans Zatanna, Elongated Man, and the Martian Manhunter, in addition to the Vixen, and newcomers Steel, **Gypsy,** and **Vibe,** the latter trio first seen here. The new team's

In the LEGENDS miniseries, Darkseid's plot to discredit Earth's heroes laid the foundation for an all-new Justice League!

headquarters is "The Bunker," a high-tech facility secreted inside an abandoned factory complex in Detroit. (JUSTICE LEAGUE OF AMERICA ANNUAL #2)

1985

February: The Justice League battles the **Overmaster** and his super-powered agents, **The Cadre** (**Black Mass, Crowbar, Fastball, Nightfall, Shatterfist,** and **Shrike**). (JUSTICE LEAGUE OF AMERICA #235)

April: DC Comics begins its 12-part CRISIS ON INFINITE EARTHS miniseries, which ultimately coalesces its super hero universes into a single, unified history. All previous alternate Earths are either destroyed or combined into this new Earth. **Blue Beetle** makes his DC debut in the very first issue.

July: Scientist **Kimiyo Hoshi** is transformed by solar radiation from the star Vega to become **Dr. Light II.** (CRISIS ON INFINITE EARTHS #4)

1986

February: **Booster Gold** (**Michael Jon Carter**) a football star from 25th-century Metropolis who has transported himself back in time to the 1980s, is introduced. (BOOSTER GOLD #1)

March: To honor the memory of his late mentor **Barry Allen, Wally West** assumes the crimson mantle of The Flash. (CRISIS ON INFINITE EARTHS #12)

June: The Bolovaxian Green Lantern **Kilowog,** later a JLI honorary member, makes his first appearance. (GREEN LANTERN CORPS #201)

Powered by the magical Tantu Totem, fashion model Mari Jiwi Macabe can channel the abilities of any animal as Vixen!

October: Superman's origins are revised and recounted once more in the pages of THE MAN OF STEEL, a six-issue miniseries beginning this month.

November: Metropolis mogul **Lex Luthor** first appears in modern continuity. (MAN OF STEEL #4)

November: DC Comics' six-part LEGENDS miniseries chronicles Darkseid's efforts to conquer Earth by turning mankind against their super-human defenders. As the storyline concludes during the following April, **Dr. Fate** leads the call for a new Justice League.

1987
January through April: Professor Ivo's revenge sees the deaths of Vibe and Steel. This four-part epic marks the end of an era and nearly 30 years of publication for JUSTICE LEAGUE OF AMERICA. (JUSTICE LEAGUE OF AMERICA #258–261)

February: Justice League International member **Dimitri Pushkin**, a.k.a. **Rocket Red #4**, debuts alongside the rest of Russia's **Rocket Red Brigade**. (GREEN LANTERN CORPS #209)

Also this month, Wonder Woman's beginnings are recast as **Princess Diana** of Themyscira is chosen to

become the Amazon messenger of peace to "Patriarch's world." (WONDER WOMAN vol. 2 #1)

March: Captain Atom is reimagined in DC Comics' CAPTAIN ATOM vol. 2 #1. U.S. Air Force General **Wade Eiling** first appears.

April: The Justice League is officially reestablished with membership including Batman, The Martian Manhunter, Dr. Fate, Black Canary, Guy Gardner, Blue Beetle, Mister Miracle, Dr. Light II, and Captain Marvel. (LEGENDS #6)

Also, Captain Marvel's origin is revamped in SHAZAM: THE NEW BEGINNING, a four-issue miniseries beginning this month.

May: The Justice League returns in an all-new series. Unscrupulous JL liaison and financier **Maxwell Lord** first appears. (JUSTICE LEAGUE #1)

June: The renegade **Lord of Order** known as **The Gray Man** is introduced. (JUSTICE LEAGUE #2)

November: Justice League becomes **Justice League International** with publication of its seventh issue. Captain Atom and **Rocket Red #7** join the League as Captain Marvel and Dr. Fate depart. (JUSTICE LEAGUE INTERNATIONAL #7)

Dr. Destiny is one of the JLA's most frequent foes. In 1989, readers of DC Comics' SANDMAN learned that Destiny's Materioptikon-powering gem was, in fact, the Dream Ruby belonging to Morpheus of the Endless.

The Demons Three
Since their debut in JUSTICE LEAGUE OF AMERICA #10, the Demons Three (Abnegazar, Rath, and Ghast) have encountered the League on several occasions in their attempts to visit chaos upon the Earth. When not wreaking havoc, the imprisoned Demons can only be freed by the power of three mystic talismans: The Silver Wheel of Nyorlath, The Green Bell of Uthool, and The Red Jar of Calythos.

Freed from his crypt, the gargantuan Rath magically transforms himself to tower over the Justice League!

December: Several dozen Justice League Embassies are established worldwide. The JLI leaves the Secret Sanctuary and takes up residence in a Metropolis-based embassy. (JUSTICE LEAGUE INTERNATIONAL #8)

1988
January–February: During DC Comics' six-issue MILLENNIUM crossover miniseries, the Justice League learn that Rocket Red #7 is a deep-cover spy for the Manhunters!

February: The JLI meets **G'nort**, a canine Green Lantern who later becomes a faithful four-legged member of **Justice League Antarctica**. (JUSTICE LEAGUE INTERNATIONAL #10)

April: After losing their Global Guardians funding, Green Flame and Icemaiden decide to join the Justice League as **Fire** and **Ice**, respectively. Readers will later learn that this Icemaiden (Tora Olafsdotter) is a different heroine from the one introduced years earlier. (JUSTICE LEAGUE INTERNATIONAL #12)

June: Fire and Ice join the Justice League as the team first runs foul of intergalactic barterer **Manga Khan** and his robotic companion **L-Ron**. (JUSTICE LEAGUE INTERNATIONAL #14)

Elsewhere, the sorceress **Circe** first appears in post-CRISIS continuity. (WONDER WOMAN vol. 2 #17)

Also, **Power Girl**'s origins are revised in a four-issue miniseries. In the Post-CRISIS DC Universe, the hard-hitting heroine was born in ancient Atlantis and sent forward in time, her suspended animation chamber patterning her powers to resemble Superman's. (POWER GIRL #1)

July: The Joker shoots and paralyzes **Barbara Gordon,** ending her crime-fighting career as **Batgirl**. Later, Barbara will become the all-seeing, all-knowing information broker known as **Oracle**. (BATMAN: THE KILLING JOKE)

August: A new Queen Bee is introduced, this time a beguiling beauty plotting her takeover of the Middle Eastern nation of Bialya. (JUSTICE LEAGUE INTERNATIONAL #14)

November: The post-CRISIS origin of the JLA is published, with Black Canary substituting for Wonder Woman and helping The Flash, J'onn J'onzz, Green Lantern, and Aquaman defeat the Appellaxian aliens. (SECRET ORIGINS vol. 3 #32)

December 1988–January 1989: The Justice League joins forces with a coalition of Earth's heroes to beat back an invasion by an alien alliance including **The Dominators, The Citadel, The Khunds, Durlans, Daxamites, Thanagarians, Psions, The G'il'Dishpan,** and **The Warlords of Okaara.** (INVASION! #1-3)

1989
January: Perennial losers **Major Disaster, Big Sur, Clock King, Multi-Man, Cluemaster,** and the self-styled **Mighty Bruce** form the hapless and hopeless Injustice League. (JUSTICE LEAGUE INTERNATIONAL #23)

Able to trigger pheromone reactions in others, the feral Crimson Fox was also an agile fighter, wielding steel claws and a whip-tailed cowl.

February: Scottish mercenary **McCulloch** takes up the reflective weaponry of **Sam Scudder,** killed during the CRISIS, to be **Mirror Master II.** (ANIMAL MAN #8)

April: **Animal Man,** The Flash, Captain Atom, Elongated Man, Power Girl, Metamorpho, Wonder Woman, and Rocket Red are the initial lineup of Justice League members setting up shop in Paris, France in JUSTICE LEAGUE EUROPE #1. The League's French liaison, **Catherine Cobert,** debuts.

Also this month, **The Huntress** makes her first appearance. (THE HUNTRESS #1)

May: JUSTICE LEAGUE INTERNATIONAL becomes

JUSTICE LEAGUE AMERICA with issue #26, a tale in which Batman meets the Huntress for the first time. She will later assume membership in the League.

September: **The Crimson Fox** – in reality, identical twins **Vivian** and **Constance D'Aramis** – first appears, later joining JLE. (JUSTICE LEAGUE EUROPE #6)

1990
March: Interplanetary designer **Mr. Nebula** and his locater-envoy, **The Scarlet Skier,** first appear. (JUSTICE LEAGUE AMERICA #36)

June: **The Extremists** (**Lord Havok, Doctor Diehard, Gorgon, Tracer,** and **Dreamslayer**), robotic villains from the same alternate dimension as Blue Jay and Silver Sorceress, first battle the Justice League. (JUSTICE LEAGUE EUROPE #15)

July: The former Injustice League adds G'nort to its roster and reforms to become the ill-fated Justice League Antarctica. Killer carnivorous penguins end this JLA's tenure. (JUSTICE LEAGUE OF AMERICA ANNUAL #4)

September: During a membership drive, **El Diablo** (Rafael Sandoval), **Starman** (Will Payton), and **Hawk** (Hank Hall) and **Dove II** (Dawn Granger) decline an offer to join the JLA. However, the New Gods Orion and Lightray enlist themselves as new members. (JUSTICE LEAGUE AMERICA #42)

October: "Average guy" **Wally Tortolini** becomes the JLA's next major foe when he wins a passel of villainous accoutrements, including Sonar's Tuning-Fork Gun, The Cavalier's sword, Quakemaster's jackhammer, Black Mass's crowbar and wristbands, Blackrock's Power Stone, and Brain Storm's high-tech helmet in a poker game. (JUSTICE LEAGUE AMERICA #43)

November: Several Justice League Europe members meet British hero **The Beefeater,** who is unfortunately denied membership in the team. (JUSTICE LEAGUE EUROPE #20)

Winter: JUSTICE LEAGUE QUARTERLY, an all-new DC Comics title debuts, introducing Booster Gold's **Conglomerate** super-team as an alternative to the Justice League. In addition to Booster, the team includes **Reverb, Praxis, Maxi-Man, Gypsy, Vapor,** and **Echo.** JLQ lasts only 17 issues before ceasing publication. (JUSTICE LEAGUE QUARTERLY #1)

Blue Beetle
Young inventor Ted Kord helped the first Blue Beetle, Daniel "Dan" Garrett, to thwart Ted's uncle Jarvis Kord's bid to take over the world. Garrett was mortally wounded in the melee, but Ted vowed to carry on his heroic work. He soon developed his own ingenious technological tricks to further the legend of the Azure Avenger!

Blue Beetle's "Bug" (top) is an all-purpose, solar-powered vehicle, capable of supersonic flight and submarine immersion.

1991
January: The patriotic **General Glory** (Joseph Jones), later a JLA member, first appears as the five-part "Glory Bound" storyline begins. (JUSTICE LEAGUE AMERICA #46)

May: JUSTICE LEAGUE AMERICA reaches its 50th issue!

August: The 14-part "Breakdowns" begins and crosses over between both Justice League America and Justice League Europe, reshaping both teams with new memberships. (JUSTICE LEAGUE AMERICA #4)

October: Super-soldier Ben Lockwood first appears as **Agent Liberty.** (SUPERMAN vol. 2 #60)

1992
February: Ray Terrill takes up the heroic mantle of his father to become **The Ray,** later a member of the Justice League Task Force. (THE RAY #1)

April: In JUSTICE LEAGUE SPECTACULAR #1, League membership is shaken up once more with the Man of Steel and Green Lantern (Hal Jordan) leading separate teams. Justice League America includes Superman, Booster Gold, Guy Gardner, Ice, Fire, and Blue Beetle. Justice League Europe now numbers Green Lantern, The Flash (Wally West), Aquaman, Dr. Light (Kimiyo Yoshi), Elongated Man, Power Girl, and Crimson Fox in its ranks.

Elsewhere, the enigmatic sorcerer **Bloodwynd** (who is actually J'onn J'onzz in disguise), a hero who will join the JLA in issue #63, debuts. (JUSTICE LEAGUE AMERICA #61)

June: The heroic **Black Condor II** first appears. (BLACK CONDOR #1)

December: The JLA first battle the creature **Doomsday,** who trounces the team's ranks and ultimately murders the Man of Steel! (JUSTICE LEAGUE AMERICA #69)

In this JLA annual, the Injustice League try to go straight – until they meet killer penguins!

1993

February: Wonder Woman, Black Condor II, The Ray, and Agent Liberty join the JLA. (JUSTICE LEAGUE AMERICA #71)

May: JUSTICE LEAGUE EUROPE sees publication of its 50th issue as the team battles **Sonar**. The following month, the series will be retitled JUSTICE LEAGUE INTERNATIONAL and continue its numbering at #51.

June: Rotating rosters of JLA associates make up the stealthy JUSTICE LEAGUE TASK FORCE, lasting 38 issues. The initial Task Force includes J'onn J'onzz, Aquaman, Nightwing, The Flash, and Gypsy. (JUSTICE LEAGUE TASK FORCE #1)

Also this month, John Henry Irons takes up sledgehammer and the mantle of Superman to become the pile-driving hero **Steel**, while the Cadmus Project creates **Superboy**, a teen clone of the Last Son of Krypton! (ADVENTURES OF SUPERMAN #500)

August: The Justice League first battles **The New Extremists: Brute, Meanstreak, Gunshot, Death Angel,** Dreamslayer, and **Cloudburst.** (JUSTICE LEAGUE AMERICA #79)

1994

January: Hal Jordan – grief-stricken over the

During the "Zero Hour" event, Wonder Woman assumed leadership of a Justice League featuring veteran and new members.

destruction of his beloved Coast City – destroys the Green Lantern Corps. (GREEN LANTERN vol. 3 #48)

February: The "New Bloods" – **Geist, Joe Public,** and **Loose Cannon** – become unofficial members of the Justice League Task Force. (JLTF #9)

March: The Justice League Task Force first encounters **The Purifiers** (**Backlash, Heatmonger, Golden Eagle, Blind Faith,** and **Iron Cross**). (JUSTICE LEAGUE TASK FORCE #10)

Also this month, freelance artist **Kyle Rayner** becomes the sole remaining Green Lantern when he is chosen by the surviving Guardian **Ganthet** to wield the last Oan power ring. (GREEN LANTERN vol. 3 #50)

April: **Grant Emerson**'s destructive metahuman powers turn him into the reluctant super-hero **Damage**! (DAMAGE #1)

July: Ice is killed in battle with the **Overmaster**. (JUSTICE LEAGUE AMERICA #90)

Also this month, **Bart Allen** – Barry Allen's grandson from the 30th century – travels to the present day to become teen speedster **Impulse**! (THE FLASH vol. 2 #92)

September: JUSTICE LEAGUE INTERNATIONAL ceases publication with issue #68.

Elsewhere, the forgotten hero **Triumph** first appears in all three Justice League titles as readers learn of the JLA's "lost" founding member, trapped in a temporal loop until now. He later joins the Justice League Task Force. (JUSTICE LEAGUE TASK FORCE #17)

Gypsy and the Bronze Tiger became lovers while members of the short-lived Justice league Task Force.

When Neron tempted DC's villains, many traded their souls for augmented abilities. The Joker swapped his immortal spirit for a box of fine cigars!

Also this month, the Amazon warrior **Artemis** assumes the mantle of Wonder Woman for a brief time when Princess Diana is considered unworthy of the role. She is later a member of the JLA alongside Diana. (WONDER WOMAN vol. 2 #90)

October: JUSTICE LEAGUE AMERICA #0 – a special issue tying into DC Comics' "Zero Hour" crossover event – features an all-new JLA lineup, comprising: Wonder Woman, The Flash, Nuklon, Crimson Fox, Metamorpho, Obsidian, Hawkman, and Fire. The new team take up residence in the Overmaster's vacated starship.

Also this month, Oliver Queen's son **Connor Hawke** first appears. (GREEN ARROW vol. 1 #0)

Elsewhere, Gypsy joins the Justice League Task Force, now including L-Ron (inhabiting the body of Despero), The Ray, Triumph, and J'onn J'onzz. (JUSTICE LEAGUE TASK FORCE #0)

November: Connor Hawke becomes a fellow Green Arrow alongside his father in the pages of GREEN ARROW vol. 1 #91!

1995

January: Captain Atom forms his own unofficial Justice League with a more proactive stance on fighting evil. His **Extreme Justice** team based within an abandoned silver mine inside Mt. Thunder includes **Amazing Man II** (Will Everett), Blue Beetle, Booster Gold, and **Maxima** as members. (EXTREME JUSTICE #0)

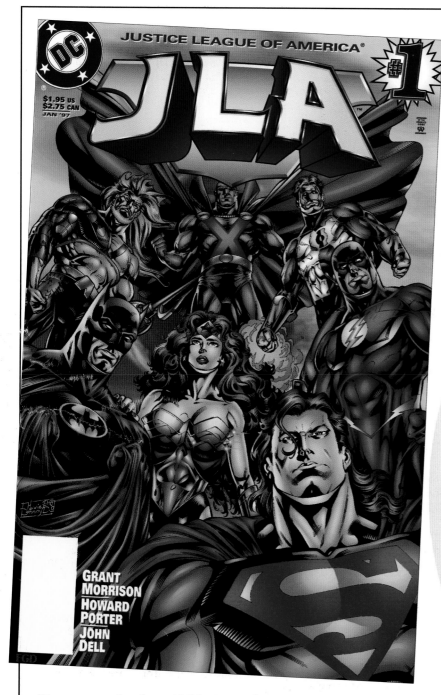

No more second-stringers! With JLA #1, the Justice League of America assembled an A-list roster of the World's Greatest Super Heroes!

March: Icemaiden takes up the deceased Ice's position in the JLA. (JUSTICE LEAGUE AMERICA #97)

April: **Blue Devil** joins Justice League America. (JUSTICE LEAGUE AMERICA #98)

June: JUSTICE LEAGUE AMERICA reaches its milestone 100th issue.

Also this month, Firestorm joins Captain Atom's Extreme Justice League. (EXTREME JUSTICE #5)

Elsewhere, Triumph's origins and return to action are chronicled in his own four-issue miniseries beginning this month. (TRIUMPH #1)

October: Fleeing an interplanetary slavelord, Zan and Jayna enter

modern DC Comics continuity and fly headlong into the path of Extreme Justice. (EXTREME JUSTICE #9)

November: **Neron**, demon ruler of the Underworld and taker of souls, is introduced. (UNDERWORLD UNLEASHED #1)

December: Thanks to the evil-enhancing demon Neron, superhuman mercenaries Merlyn, **Deadshot**, **Bolt**, **Chiller**, and **Deadline** form **The Killer Elite**. (JUSTICE LEAGUE AMERICA #106)

1996
August: JUSTICE LEAGUE AMERICA ends its remarkable nine-year run at issue #113.

Also this month, DC Comics readers are introduced to **Dr. Curt Falconer**, better known as **Aztek**! (AZTEK: THE ULTIMATE MAN #1)

And elsewhere, Triumph quits the Justice League as JUSTICE LEAGUE TASK FORCE #37 ends that title's tenure.

September: The first issue of JUSTICE LEAGUE: A MIDSUMMER'S NIGHTMARE is published, pitting the team against the enigmatic **Knowman**. This three-issue miniseries lays the groundwork for the return of the JLA as a team of DC's heaviest hitters: Superman, Batman, Wonder Woman, The Martian Manhunter, Green Lantern, The Flash, and Aquaman.

November: The "Warbringer" later known as **Mageddon** is first mentioned in a warning to the reformed JLA from Knowman. (JUSTICE LEAGUE: A MIDSUMMER'S NIGHTMARE #3)

1997
January: The JLA hits the ground running with a pantheon of its most powerful members defending Earth from **The Hyperclan** (**Protex**, **A-Mortal**, **Züm**, **Fluxus**, **Primaid**, **Tronix**, **Armek**, and **Zenturion**). In reality, the alien team are **White Martians** bent on planetary domination. Metamorpho sacrifices himself to save his fellow former team members (Icemaiden, Nuklon, and Obsidian) and is later buried after being declared "inert." (JLA #1)

April: After defeating the White Martians, the JLA erects its latest headquarters, **The Watchtower**, on the surface of the Moon. (JLA #4)

May: The new JLA conducts its first membership drive, inducting **Tomorrow Woman**, an android "mole" created by villainous scientists T. O. Morrow and Professor Ivo. (JLA #5)

Also this month, Aztek joins the JLA. During the ceremony, he pledges his oath of allegiance upon the cloak of the Crimson Avenger, DC Comics' first official costumed super hero. (AZTEK: THE ULTIMATE MAN #10)

Zauriel brought the rage of angels down upon the JLA. Later, the winged hero filled a feathered seat in the JLA left vacant by Hawkman.

June: The JLA meets the fallen angel **Zauriel**, later a member of the team. The hellish Neron encourages the Demons Three to rip the Moon from its orbit while he unleashes The Key from catatonic slumber. (JLA #6)

July: The JLA is faced with **Asmodel**, renegade angel from Heaven's Bull Host. The Key strikes with a new look and *modus operandi*. (JLA #7)

August: Green Arrow Connor Hawke's JLA induction ceremony is interrupted by the Key and his Key-Men! (JLA #8)

September: The new JLA's origin is recounted as the **Star-Conqueror** attempts to turn Earth's humans into its mindless drones! (JLA SECRET FILES #1)

October: Lex Luthor forms a new Injustice Gang to thwart the JLA. This incarnation includes Luthor, Circe, **Ocean Master**, The Joker, Mirror Master, and **J'emm**, a Saturnian hero under Luthor's thrall. Luthor's acquisition of the **Worlogog** (or "Philosopher's Stone") leads to Darkseid's domination of Earth in the future. (JLA #10)

Ironically, no JLA member can know that former teammate Hal Jordan lives on as the otherworldly Spectre!

DC One Million
As Montevideo, Uruguay was enshrouded in nuclear fire, the JLA was nowhere to be found! Invited to the 853rd century by its own descendants, the League took part in a galaxy-wide celebration to welcome back the first Superman from self-imposed exile in the sun. But little did the JLA or its futuristic successors in Justice Legion A realize that the tyrant sun Solaris plotted with Vandal Savage to murder the Prime-Superman with a fragment of kryptonite!

The members of Justice Legion A patrolled their own planets. Starman (second from left) was the guardian of Solaris. He betrayed the team to aid the stellar supercomputer's schemes!

The visiting heroes of Justice Legion A did their best to provide disaster relief in Montevideo, but the android Hourman unwittingly carried Solaris's techno-plague and spread a mind-destroying virus !

December: Adrift in time, Aquaman, The Flash, and Green Lantern meet the brobdingnagian champions of **Wonderworld** and first encounter the "machine colony" **Hourman**, an android from the 853rd century destined to become a hero in the 20th, a friend to the JLA, and a member of the JSA. The threat of **Solaris** is first mentioned. (JLA #12)

1998
January: DC Comics publishes the first installment of the 12-part JLA: YEAR ONE, chronicling the World's Greatest Super Heroes seminal adventures. The evil genetics-tampering organization **Locus** first appears here. (JLA: YEAR ONE #1)

Elsewhere, the future Apokoliptic occupation of Earth ends when the surviving JLA members, including Batman and the Atom, sacrifice their lives to end Darkseid's tyranny for all time. The Flash, Green Lantern, and Aquaman return to the present and prevent the destruction of the Worlogog, which precipitated this dark destiny.
(JLA #14)

Also this month, the hero hunter **Prometheus** first appears.
(PROMETHEUS #1)

March: As the JLA announces its new inductees Orion, Big Barda, The Huntress, Zauriel, Steel, and Oracle,

Tomorrow Woman, who was built to fool the JLA into believing her a true heroine, exceeded her makers' evil expectations by proving to be more human than they anticipated!

Prometheus infiltrates the JLA and attempts to destroy the team members one-by-one. This issue features detailed blueprints of the JLA Watchtower. (JLA #16)

May: The probability-altering scientist **Julian September** first appears. He is later killed by the events spilling out of his Engine of Chance. (JLA #18)

June: JLA: TOMORROW WOMAN, a one-shot "Girlfrenzy" crossover, provides additional background on the android Tomorrow Woman and her short tenure with the JLA.

July: **The Justice Experience**, a team of super heroes operating in the interim between the JSA's retirement and the formation of the JLA, is introduced. This group, active during the late 1960s and early 1970s, included **The Acro-Bat**, **Mister Action**, **The Manx**, **Major Flashback**, **Song Bird**, and **The Bronze Wraith**. (CHASE #6)

September: Robin, Superboy, and Impulse take up residence in the JLA's former mountainous Secret Sanctuary as the adventures of YOUNG JUSTICE begin.

November – December: During DC Comics' epic ONE MILLION crossover, the Justice League joins forces with their counterparts from the distant future in **Justice Legion A** to defeat the stellar supercomputer named Solaris! (DC ONE MILLION #1–2)

December: The JLA meets the U.S. Military's homegrown heroes, **The Ultramarine Corps** (4-D, Flux, Pulse-8, and **Warmaker One**).
(JLA #24)

1999
January: General Wade Eiling transplants his brain into the body of the indestructible Shaggy Man! Calling himself The General, he shaves the long hair from his mighty new form into the very model of military megalomania. (JLA #25)

March: The Atom resumes part-time membership in the JLA after aiding the team defeat Amazo, now powered by every League member, past to present. (JLA #27)

June: Malevolent imp **Quisp** remakes himself as **Qwsp**, engineering a war between Johnny Thunder's Thunderbolt and another Earthbound third-dimensional imp in a battle uniting the JLA with the reestablished JSA! (JLA #30)

July: After aiding Qwsp, the down-and-out turncoat hero Triumph receives a crystalline comeuppance from the Spectre and is transformed into a statue of solid ice. (JLA #31)

August: The Justice Society of America returns to active duty in the pages of the all-new JSA #1!

October: Zazzala, The Queen Bee, is reintroduced as Lex Luthor convenes a deadlier Injustice Gang with the General and Prometheus in its roguish roster. Also this issue, JLA readers first glimpse Mageddon's cyclopean "Remote Sender." (JLA #34)

December: Earth suddenly erupts in global violence as "World War III" begins. (JLA #36)

Also this year, **Kobra** displaces the psyches of several JLA members from their respective bodies in his continued quest for world domination. In defeat, Kobra finds himself haunted by the deceased spirit of his good twin, Jason Burr. (JLA: FOREIGN BODIES)

During THE SILVER AGE, the Injustice Gang pulled a super-powered switcheroo, trading bodies with the JLA for a costumed crime spree!

The mystic Mordru's murder of original Sandman Wesley Dodds and other "Golden Age" heroes led to the formation of a new cross-generational JSA!

2000

January: The "Ultimate Warbringer" Mageddon is first seen in all its devastating glory while Luthor bombs the JLA's lunar Watchtower. Zauriel's mortal body is destroyed. (JLA #37)

March: Batman summarily revokes the Huntress's JLA membership after she attempts to kill Prometheus for his heinous crimes. (JLA #39)

May: Aztek detonates his armor and blows himself up in a heroic, but vain, attempt to stop Mageddon in the conclusion to the "World War III" storyline. With Mageddon halted, Orion and Big Barda depart the League. (JLA #41)

July: Beginning in this month's opening installment of the four-part "Tower of Babel" storyline, the JLA battle Batman's arch-foe Rā's al Ghūl, who uses the Dark Knight's own secret counter-measures against his fellow League members to incapacitate them. (JLA #43)

Elsewhere, a pivotal adventure from the JLA's early years is revealed in DC Comics' SILVER AGE crossover, which introduces Lex Luthor's Injustice League (Luthor, Felix Faust,

Interestingly, it took nearly 30 years for the JLA to finally encounter Batman's most powerful arch-foe, the immortal eco-terrorist Rā's al Ghūl!

Mr. Element, Dr. Light, **Black Manta**, Chronos, **Catwoman**, and Sinestro) and the universal threat of **Agamemno**! (SILVER AGE #1)

November: The JLA grapple with the universe's very first living beings, **The Quantum Mechanics**, in the oversized JLA: HEAVEN'S LADDER one-shot.

Also this month, **The Queen of Fables** turns fairy-tale fiction into fatal fact in her first battle with the Justice League! (JLA #47)

December: **The Advance Man**, a forward agent reconnoitering Earth for potential alien invaders, first appears. (JLA: SECRET FILES #3)

Also this year, in the hardcover JLA: EARTH 2, the Justice Leaguers pay a visit to the anti-matter universe and find themselves face-to-face with the "world's gravest super-villains" the **Crime Syndicate of Amerika**!

2001

January: The Justice League of America celebrates the publication of JLA #50 as the team faces Dr. Destiny once more!

March: During the six-part "JUSTICE LEAGUES" 5th-week crossover, the Advance Man succeeds in shattering the JLA, forcing the individual team members to form their own unique Justice Leagues to forestall an alien invasion. Superman and the Martian Manhunter's Justice League of Aliens includes **Starfire**, **Lobo**, Orion, **Warrior** (Guy Gardner), and Starman. (JLA: JUSTICE LEAGUE OF ALIENS #1)

Different Incarnations

JLA: INCARNATIONS addressed some thorny continuity conflicts in the post-CRISIS DC Universe, including establishing that the JSA's Hawkman and Hawkgirl in fact joined the League as elder liaisons between teams. Batman's membership was enacted after he aided the League in fending off the intelligent T-Rex Fire-Eye. And in current canon, the JLA satellite was destroyed by aliens known as "The Debris," rather than war-mongering Green Martians.

Wonder Woman's Justice League of Amazons includes Zatanna, Power Girl, Big Barda, Supergirl, and The Huntress. (JLA: JUSTICE LEAGUE OF AMAZONS #1)

Aquaman's Justice League of Atlantis includes his wife Mera, Power Girl, Arion, mermaid Lori Lemaris, and Tempest. (JLA: JUSTICE LEAGUE OF ATLANTIS #1)

Meanwhile, Batman's unorthodox Justice League of Arkham includes rogues Catwoman, The Joker, Poison Ivy, The Ventriloquist and Scarface, and The Riddler. (JLA: JUSTICE LEAGUE OF ARKHAM #1)

April: As the JLA first encounter the alien "sentergy" known as **Id**, a creation of the Sixth Dimensional Cathexis, the team members' heroic personas are separated from their civilian alter egos! (JLA #51)

May: The JLA Watchtower is upgraded by the League members to its current design. (JLA #52)

Also this month, the four-issue JLA: BLACK BAPTISM miniseries begins, pitting the Justice League against the hit men known as **The Diablos**, demonic agents of Felix Faust! Fortunately, the team finds arcane aid from **The Sentinels of Magic!**

July: Each major grouping of the JLA is spotlighted as the seven-issue JLA: INCARNATIONS minseries begins. This first issue pits the team and their JSA forebears against the mystical menace Wotan.

August: The JLA's first encounter with Gorilla Grodd is chronicled. (JLA: INCARNATIONS #2)

Elsewhere, the White Martians escape their imprisonment as the four-part "Terra Incognita" begins. (JLA #55)

September: Kobra launches his first major assault against the JLA in this untold tale from the team's past. (JLA: INCARNATIONS #3)

Also this month, as the galaxy-spanning **Imperiex War** spills upon Earth, Aquaman and Atlantis are apparently disintegrated as the King of the Seven Seas fights valiantly to spare his underwater kingdom. Aquaman is officially listed as "Missing in Action." (JLA: OUR WORLDS AT WAR)

October: JLA readers are introduced to aquatic menaces **Captain Squidd** and **Killer Whale**, as well as the alien attacker **Koll**. (JLA: INCARNATIONS #4)

Elsewhere this year, the Justice League is unable to stop a densely populated alien city from crashing to Earth in California. Known as **Haven**, the metropolis introduces scores of new superpowered characters to the DC Universe. (JLA/HAVEN: ARRIVAL)

2002

January: DC Comics launches JUSTICE LEAGUE ADVENTURES, a series based on the Cartoon Network's smash hit *Justice League* animated series. This League includes Batman, Superman, Wonder Woman, Hawkgirl, The Martian Manhunter, The Flash (Wally West), and Green Lantern (John Stewart) in its ranks.

Also this month, Plastic Man tells the story of how **Santa Claus** defeated the demon Neron and joined the JLA! (JLA #60)

Aquaman is now exiled from the oceans as a result of catastrophic decisions he made while Atlantis was trapped in the past.

February: JLA #61 includes a sneak preview of **The Power Company** a super-hero team and legal firm whose staff has had personal encounters with the Justice League!

March: The Justice League of America battles the elemental mystic **Rama Khan**, guardian of the Eden-like Jarhanpur. In the ensuing conflict, Wonder Woman's unbreakable Golden Lasso of Truth is torn apart! (JLA #62)

June: In "Bouncing Baby Boy," Batman learns that Plastic Man has a son, the 10-year-old, shape-changing **Luke McDunnagh**. Plas enlists the Batman to help scare juvenile delinquent Luke to go straight in this adventure, which stars only the Dark Knight and his "Dark Nut" teammate. (JLA #65)

Early August: The seven-part "The Obsidian Age: The Hunt for Aquaman" begins as the Justice League faces an ancient evil in their search for the lost King of the Sea! (JLA #69)

Early September: With their predecessors believed destroyed, a new JLA convenes as the search for Aquaman continues! (JLA #71)

Late September: At long last, Aquaman returns! (JLA #72)

INDEX

JLA

ACKNOWLEDGMENTS

Dorling Kindersley would like to thank the following DC artists and writers for their contributions to this book:

Christian Alamy, Marlo Alquiza, Murphy Anderson, Derec Aucoin, Michael Bair, Darryl Banks, Scott Beatty, Doug Braithwaite, Sal Buscema, Buzz, John Byrne, Sergio Cariello, Keith Champagne, Saleem Crawford, CrisCross, Alan Davis, Adam DeKraker, John Dell, Bob Dvorak, Dale Eaglesham, Scot Eaton, Steve Epting, Rich Faber, Mark Farmer, John Floyd, Gary Frank, George Freeman, James Fry, Ron Garney, Drew Geraci, Dick Giordano, Al Gordon, Peter Grau, Mick Gray, Devin Grayson, Dan Green, Tom Grindberg, Tom Grummett, Butch Guice, Steven Harris, Andrew Hennessy, Phil Hester, Don Hillsman, Bryan Hitch, Jon Holdredge, Richard Horie, Tanya Horie, Stuart Immonen, Georges Jeanty, Oscar Jimenez, Phil Jimenez, Arnie Jorgensen, Dan Jurgens, Kano, Joe Kelly, Karl Kesel, Ray Kryssing, Greg Land, Andy Lanning, Bud LaRosa, Mark Lipka, Aaron Lopresti, Ray McCarthy, Ed McGuinness, Mike McKone, Bob McLeod, Dev Madan, Kevin Maguire, Doug Mahnke, Tom Mandrake, Jeanty Martin, Kenny Martinez, José Marzan Jr., David Meikis, Mark Millar, Mike Miller, Mark Morales, Rags Morales, Grant Morrison, Todd Nauck, Paul Neary, Tom Nguyen, Philip Noto, Kevin Nowlan, Ariel Olivetti, Jerry Ordway, John Ostrander, Mark Pajarillo, Jimmy Palmiotti, Yanick Paquette, Ande Parks, Paul Pelletier, Mark Pennington, Andrew Pepoy, George Perez, Howard Porter, Mark Probst, Frank Quitely, Pablo Raimondi, Rodney Ramos, Norm Rapmund, Cliff Rathburn, Robin Riggs, Darick Robertson, Roger Robinson, Hannibal Rodriguez, Prentis Rollins, Dave Ross, Bernard Sachs, Steven Sadowski, Javier Saltares, Steve Scott, Bart Sears, Mike Sekowsky, Val Semeiks, Cam Smith, Ray Snyder, Claude St. Aubin, Brian Stelfreeze, John Stokes, Lary Stucker, David Tanguay, Ty Templeton, Angel Unzueta, Ethan Van Sciver, Dexter Vines, Mark Waid, Chip Wallace, J. H. Williams III, Anthony Williams, Chuck Wojtkiewicz, Walden Wong.

The writer would especially like to thank the following for their invaluable help in producing this book: Jennifer Myskowski, Jaye Gardner, Alastair Dougall, Robert Perry, Steve Korté, Dan Raspler, Stephen Wacker, Georg Brewer, Paul Kupperberg, Tom Grindberg, Mark Waid, Robert Greenberger, Mark Schultz, Chuck Dixon, Dave Romeo Jr., Jeff Rabkin, and the many comic book writers and artists who have chronicled the inspiring and unforgettable exploits of the World's Greatest Super Heroes.

Dorling Kindersley would also like to thank the following: Jaye Gardner, Steve Korté at DC Comics; Julia March for editorial assistance; Hilary Bird for the index.